How to Keep Score in Business

How to Keep Score in Business

Accounting and Financial Analysis
for the Non-Accountant

Second Edition

Robert Follett

Vice President, Publisher: Tim Moore
Associate Publisher and Director of Marketing: Amy Neidlinger
Executive Editor: Jeanne Glasser
Editorial Assistant: Pamela Boland
Senior Marketing Manager: Julie Phifer
Assistant Marketing Manager: Megan Graue
Cover Designer: Chuti Prasertsith
Managing Editor: Kristy Hart
Project Editor: Anne Goebel
Copy Editor: Gayle Johnson
Proofreader: Linda Seifert
Indexer: Lisa Stumpf
Compositor: Nonie Ratcliff
Manufacturing Buyer: Dan Uhrig

This book is sold with the understanding that neither the author nor the publisher is engaged in rendering legal, accounting, or other professional services or advice by publishing this book. Each individual situation is unique. Thus, if legal or financial advice or other expert assistance is required in a specific situation, the services of a competent professional should be sought to ensure that the situation has been evaluated carefully and appropriately. The author and the publisher disclaim any liability, loss, or risk resulting directly or indirectly from the use or application of any of the contents of this book.

FT Press offers excellent discounts on this book when ordered in quantity for bulk purchases or special sales. For more information, please contact U.S. Corporate and Government Sales, 1-800-382-3419, corpsales@pearsontechgroup.com. For sales outside the U.S., please contact International Sales at

international@pearson.com.

Company and product names mentioned herein are the trademarks or registered trademarks of their respective owners.

ISBN-10: 0-13-284925-9
ISBN-13: 978-0-13-284925-8

Pearson Education LTD.
Pearson Education Australia PTY, Limited.
Pearson Education Singapore, Pte. Ltd.
Pearson Education Asia, Ltd.
Pearson Education Canada, Ltd.
Pearson Educatión de Mexico, S.A. de C.V.
Pearson Education—Japan
Pearson Education Malaysia, Pte. Ltd.

Library of Congress Cataloging-in-Publication Data:

Follett, Robert J. R.
 How to keep score in business : accounting and financial analysis for the
non-accountant / Robert
Follett. -- 2nd ed.
   p. cm.
Includes index.
 ISBN-13: 978-0-13-284925-8 (pbk. : alk. paper)
 ISBN-10: 0-13-284925-9 (pbk. : alk. paper)
 1. Financial statements. 2. Accounting. I. Title.
 HF5681.B2F59 2012
 657--dc23
                          2011031215

Contents

Acknowledgments

The author acknowledges all the accountants, CPAs, and financial analysts who helped make this book possible. There are those who embarrassed the author by highlighting his ignorance. They stimulated the research and thought that led to this book. There are also those who served as helpful mentors, kindly critics, and reviewers of the book's contents. Of course, I am responsible for the entire contents, and any errors are mine alone. But the book would not have happened without the help of accounting and finance professionals too numerous to name.

About the Author

Robert Follett never had a course in accounting or finance. But as he moved into corporate management, he had to learn about these subjects in order to be successful. He learned the hard way.

Keeping score using accounting and financial analysis is an important skill that many who move up from nonmanagement positions don't have. Follett wanted to help others avoid the dumb mistakes he made. That's why *How to Keep Score in Business* came to life.

Before the book was written, Follett undertook much study and then presented seminars, workshops, and short courses for new managers. These helped him hone the book's contents.

Follett began his career as a very junior editor in a publishing company. He rose through both editorial and sales positions to become president. Then he became chairman of a large, multidivision company. His business career spans over 60 years—years in which knowing the basics of accounting and financial analysis has been critical.

Follett is the author of seven other books. He teaches university classes, mainly for young people with no knowledge of accounting or finance who will need this knowledge as their careers develop. He works with various charitable organizations and continues his involvement in business.

1

Introduction

The purpose of this book is to teach you the fundamentals of keeping score in business. You will learn the basic workings of the accounting system. When you are through, you will be able to read, understand, discuss, and use a balance sheet, an income statement, and other statements found in financial reports. You will know something about various tools for analyzing financial reports and investment opportunities. You will have a basic vocabulary of the important terms used in accounting. You will be able to talk with more confidence to accountants, auditors, financial analysts, budget directors, controllers, treasurers, bankers, brokers, and lots of other people who use accounting jargon.

This book will not make you an accountant. But it will help you talk with accountants. This book will not teach you to keep the books for a company. But it will help you understand the financial reports produced by bookkeepers and accountants.

This is a book for non-accountants. It was written by a non-accountant. This book aims to make you successful in business despite your lack of formal accounting education or experience.

To get the most out of this book, you need three things. You need to keep paper and pencil beside you as you read. You need a calculator (or a good head for computation). Any cheap, simple calculator that can add, subtract, multiply, and divide will do. If you don't have one, I strongly recommend that you get one. Finally, you will need some time to get the most out of this book.

This is not a long book. But it will repay close attention. Some of the concepts are confusing. Some of the computations are a bit complex. There is nothing here that a good high school student cannot understand and handle. But it will take time. The time you spend will be repaid with a basic understanding of business accounting.

The title of this book is *How to Keep Score in Business*. In business, the score is kept in dollars. The system of accounting provides the rules for keeping score. Some people don't understand keeping score in football. They get mixed up about touchdowns, safeties, field goals, and points after. And when there is talk of the number of sacks, percentage completions, and yards per carry, they go blank.

A lot of people don't understand keeping score in business. They get mixed up about profits, assets, cash flow, and return on investment. Discounted cash flow, current ratio, and book value per share leave them blank. This book fills in some of the blanks.

Knowing how to keep score in business is essential to moving up in management. That's why seminars on accounting and finance for nonfinancial managers are among the most popular. That's why courses on this topic are offered at hundreds of colleges and continuing-education centers. That's why hundreds of books have been published on this topic.

However, most of the seminars, courses, and books suffer from one major problem.

They are put together by accountants.

Most accountants know too much to explain the business score-keeping system to the non-accountant.

I am not an accountant. I started my business career in sales. Then I had a lot to do with product development. I was the president of a large company. I became chairman of an even larger company. Along the way I had to learn about financial accounting the hard way. I have worked with accountants, auditors, bankers, treasurers, and controllers. These experts often flimflammed me with accounting lingo I didn't understand. I was made to look like a fool because somebody with an accounting degree exposed my ignorance. I've made almost every dumb mistake that a manager with no financial or accounting background can make.

But over many years in business I finally learned something about the accounting system. Now I can keep score along with the best. I don't know everything. But I know enough to be a good manager who can use financial information.

If you study this book carefully, I'll give you many years of hard knocks and dumb mistakes distilled into a relatively few pages. When you're finished studying this book, you will be well on your way to mastering an indispensable management skill. You will know the basic system for keeping score in business. You will understand the major elements of financial accounting.

Here is how the rest of the book is organized:

In the remainder of this chapter you will learn why this book is about keeping score. You will see that accounting scores are not the same as spendable dollars. This key concept will underlie much of the rest of the book.

Chapter 2 is a glossary of key financial terms. Here you will find definitions of the key words and phrases most often used by accountants. These are practical definitions that will help you develop the essential vocabulary you need for communication. You will want to refer to this glossary often—as you use the rest of the book and later, when you deal with accountants and financial reports.

Chapter 3 introduces you to the balance sheet. This is a statement of a company's financial position at one point in time. It is a basic financial report. In this chapter you will invest in the Acme Widget Company.

Chapter 4 tells more about the balance sheet. It gives you insight into what is shown and what is *not* shown. You will learn some useful methods of analyzing balance sheet information. Some valuable information never appears on any financial report. This will be discussed in this chapter.

Chapter 5 completes the presentation on the balance sheet. When you are finished with this chapter, you will have completed the most difficult part of the book—difficult because it introduces you to many new concepts and ideas. These will make it much easier for you to handle the chapters that follow. Then you will be better able to handle real-life experiences with financial reports.

We turn to the income statement in Chapter 6. This financial report summarizes a company's operations over a period of time. The last line of the income statement is the famous "bottom line." You will learn what income statements show and what they hide. Various ways of analyzing income statements are introduced. A brief section shows the reconciliation between the income statement and the balance sheet—how they connect.

Chapter 7 discusses return on investment. Several methods of computing return on investment are presented. Return on investment is an excellent way to evaluate company performance or analyze possible investments or acquisitions. You will learn how to use this tool.

The statement of changes in financial position is presented and analyzed in Chapter 8. Using this statement will help you see how funds flow into, through, and out of a company. It reveals some of the things that are not too clear on the balance sheet or income statement.

Chapter 9 teaches you one method of making a cash flow budget. This is an especially valuable management tool. With it you can plan ahead and avoid the embarrassment of running out of cash, even when sales are good. (It can happen.)

Chapter 10 introduces a variety of other analysis ratios and tools. Some are valuable to managers, others to lenders, and still others to investors. I will caution you about the limitations of these ratios and tools. No substitute has yet been devised for common sense.

What will you have learned when you finish this book? Chapter 11 is the summary chapter. It briefly recaps all the major ideas presented in the preceding ten chapters.

This book has no pinup pictures. But it does have a lot of figures. You will find many of them in the tables and illustrations and in the Appendixes. Appendix A summarizes the most important details of Acme Widget Company. Appendix B is a table of present values. You will learn how to use this valuable analysis tool in Chapter 7. You will want to use it frequently thereafter. The book ends with an index, where you can quickly look up things as you work with financial reports and accountants.

Have fun! Number crunching and massaging of figures can be an enjoyable pastime, even if you have no formal training. This book should give you enough information so that you can crunch and massage with anyone.

The First Lesson: Scores Are Not Real Dollars

Basically, accounting is simple. Lots of people are accountants who aren't as smart as you are. Of course, the Internal Revenue Service, the Financial Accounting Standards Board, the Securities and Exchange Commission, and other organizations have made a basically simple system more complicated. To be a good manager you need to know only the basics. Let's begin with the most basic of basics—the bottom line.

When people talk about the bottom line, they usually mean the last line of an income statement, which is labeled "Net Profit After Taxes" or "Net Income." This is the amount of money a business has to spend, right?

Wrong! Dead wrong.

The bottom line, net profit after taxes, is just a score. The business may have many more actual dollars to spend than the bottom-line figure shows. Or it may have a lot fewer dollars to spend. The bottom line is a score. Don't confuse the score with real money. For a long time I did. This led to a lot of dumb mistakes.

Learn this lesson, and learn it well. The numbers you see on financial reports are scores in the game of business. They usually do not represent real, spendable dollars. In the remainder of this book you will be shown why this is so. You will also see how to figure out how many real spendable dollars a business has or is likely to have in the future.

Let's carry this further. You get a sales report. It shows the number of dollars of sales. Can the money from these sales be spent? No! In most businesses, sales figures are scores. The actual money will be unavailable until later, when the customers pay their bills.

You get a purchasing report. It shows how many dollars worth of goods have been purchased and put into stock. Does that mean those dollars are spent and gone? No! In most businesses this is a score. The actual dollars are not paid to the suppliers of the goods until sometime later.

And so it goes with most financial reports. These reports show scores. Scores are not the same thing as real, spendable dollars.

The Accrual Method

It is time to turn to a diabolical accounting invention—the accrual method.

Individuals keep track of cash. In fact, the IRS directs individuals to keep track of their cash expenditures and cash revenues for tax purposes. This means you don't have any revenue until you have cash in hand (or could have it). Just because someone owes you the money doesn't mean you have any revenue.

The same thing goes for your personal expenditures. If you want to take a deduction for a medical expense on your tax return, you actually have to pay the bill with a check or currency. Just because you visited the doctor and he sent you a bill is not enough to get you a tax deduction. Cash has to change hands.

None of this is true in business. In business, we use the accrual method of accounting, not the cash method.

If you used the accrual method, you would record your revenue whenever it was first owed to you, not when it was paid. You would record your expenditure when you got the doctor's bill, not when you paid it.

The business world offers similar examples of the accrual method. A sales transaction is recorded when the company makes up an invoice for the sale. The dollars are recorded on the financial reports at that time, even though the customer may actually pay days or weeks or months later—or never.

The same thing happens in reverse when a company buys something. As soon as the company gets the invoice for the goods or services it is buying, the cost is recorded in the company's financial records. The dollars involved in the purchase will show on financial reports, even though the company may not pay those dollars for 30 or 300 days.

These are examples of the workings of the accrual system. Transactions enter the financial records as soon as they take place, not when the cash involved with the transaction changes hands. It is quite possible for a company to report big profits and be broke—unable to come up with enough cash to buy a cup of coffee. Conversely, a company may show a loss on its financial reports even though it put cash in the bank.

The accrual method of business accounting guarantees that financial reports show scores, not real, spendable dollars.

But Scores Are Important

Before we leave this topic, let me offer a word of caution. Don't think that scores are unimportant because they don't represent real dollars. Jobs are lost, promotions are won, raises are given, companies bought and sold on the basis of financial scores. You want to have good scores in business, even if they don't reflect the true cash status. Good scores produce winners in business just as good scores produce winners in sports.

In the rest of this book, you will learn some ways to improve the scores.

2

Glossary of Key Financial Accounting Terms

The biggest problem most people have with an unfamiliar area is the vocabulary. They feel uneasy because they don't know the jargon. Professionals overwhelm the amateurs with confusing words and phrases.

This chapter gives practical definitions of 142 terms used in financial accounting. If you have some grasp of these words and phrases, you will be able to deal with financial accounting and accountants.

In some respects this is the most important chapter. That's why it is near the beginning of the book, rather than in the back where glossaries are usually found. Being able to cope with these terms will make the rest of the book much easier. It will also make your dealings with financial people and their reports much easier.

Read through this chapter quickly. Then go through it again more carefully. As you go on to later chapters, come back to this glossary whenever you need to refresh your understanding. Use the glossary when you need to interpret memos, bulletins, articles, or presentations by accountants, financial analysts, bankers, and so on. If you have a good grasp of the jargon, you will be amazed at how well you can hold your own in discussions. Knowing the accounting vocabulary is a major factor in management success.

Glossary

80/20 rule
A general rule of thumb in business that says that 20 percent of the items produce 80 percent of the action. Twenty percent of the product line generates 80 percent of the sales, 20 percent of the sales force produces 80 percent of the orders, 20 percent of the customers produce 80 percent of the complaints, and so on. Of course, this rule is inaccurate, but it does reflect the often-proven truth that nothing is evenly distributed; there is concentration. In evaluating any business situation be sure you find out which small group produces the major share of the transactions you are concerned with. Looking at things with the 80/20 rule in mind will sharpen your perceptions greatly.

account
A record of financial transactions. Usually refers to a specific category or type of transaction, such as a travel expense account or purchase account.

accountant
A person who is usually trained to understand and maintain financial records. (See *bookkeeper*, *CPA*.)

accounting
A system for keeping score in business using dollars. Sometimes how people refer to an accounting department where the score is kept.

accounting period
The period of time over which profits are calculated. Normal accounting periods are months, quarters, and years (either calendar or fiscal).

accounts payable
Amounts owed by a company for the goods or services it has purchased from outside suppliers. (See *liability—current*.)

accounts receivable
Amounts owed to a company by its customers. (See *assets—current*.)

accrual basis, system, or method
An accounting system that records revenues and expenses at the time the transaction occurs, not at the time cash changes hands. If you buy a coat and charge it, the store records or accrues the sale when

you walk out with the coat, not when you pay your bill. Cash basis accounting is used by individuals. Accrual basis accounting is used by most businesses.

accruals, accrued expenses

A current liability that is an expense incurred but not yet paid for. Salaries are a good example. Employees earn or accrue salaries each hour they work. When they are paid, the accrued expense of their earned salaries is eliminated.

aging

A process in which accounts receivable are sorted by age. A debt that is only a few days old is a lot better than one that has not been paid for a year. Aging often sorts accounts receivable into current (less than 30 days after the sale was made), 30 to 60 days old, 60 to 120 days old, and so on. Aging permits collection efforts to focus on accounts that are long overdue. Aging also helps determine the amounts that should be put into allowances or reserves for bad debts or doubtful accounts. In valuing a company, the accounts receivable should be aged. A preponderance of old accounts may indicate that the accounts receivable asset is worth much less than is shown on the books.

amortize

To charge a regular portion of an expenditure over a fixed period of time. For example, if something cost $100 and is to be amortized over ten years, the financial reports will show an expense of $10 per year for ten years. If the cost were not amortized, the entire $100 would show up as an expense in the year the expenditure was made. (See *depreciation, expenditure, expense.*)

appreciation

An increase in value. If a machine cost $1,000 last year and is now worth $1,200, it has appreciated in value by $200. The opposite of depreciation.

asset

Something of value owned by a business. An asset may be cash; or a physical property, such as a building; or an object, such as a stock certificate; or it may be a right, such as the right to use a patented process.

Current assets can be expected to turn into cash within a year or less. Current assets include cash, marketable securities, accounts receivable, and inventory.

Fixed assets cannot be quickly turned into cash without interfering with business operations. Fixed assets include land, buildings, machinery, equipment, furniture, and long-term investments.

Intangible assets are things such as patents, copyrights, trademarks, licenses, franchises, and other kinds of rights or things of value to a company that are not physical objects. These assets may be the important ones a company owns. Often they are not shown on financial reports.

audit
A careful review of financial records to verify their accuracy.

auditor
A person who performs an audit.

average collection period
The average number of days required to collect accounts receivable. Average collection period = accounts receivable ÷ sales × 365. Average collection periods differ from industry to industry. When a company's average collection period gets longer, this indicates a problem. Customers may be getting into financial difficulty. Collection efforts may be lagging. Product quality or service may have declined to the point that customers have many complaints that must be resolved before they will pay. Or perhaps more liberal credit terms have to be given to induce customers to buy a sagging product line. The average collection period over the past several years should always be computed when analyzing a company.

bad debt
An amount owed to a company that will not be paid. An account becomes a bad debt when the company recognizes that the debt won't be paid. Sometimes bad debts are written off when recognized. Other times a reserve is set up to provide for possible bad debts. This is usually called reserve or allowance for bad debts, or reserve or allowance for doubtful accounts. The write-off of a bad debt is an expense. Any addition to the reserve or allowance is also an expense. When

there is a reserve or allowance, recognition of an actual bad debt will not result in an expense, because it has already been allowed for in expenses. Unrecognized bad debts for which no allowance or reserve has been set up are an important factor to consider in evaluating a company's value.

balance sheet

A statement of a company's financial position at a single, specific time (often at the close of business on the last day of the year). The balance sheet normally lists all assets on the left side or the top of the sheet. All liabilities and capital are listed on the right side or bottom of the sheet. The total of all the numbers on the left side or top must equal or balance the total of all the numbers on the right side or bottom. A balance sheet balances according to this equation: assets = liabilities + capital.

bond

A written record of a debt payable more than a year in the future. It shows the amount of the debt, due date, interest, and other conditions.

book

A record of financial transactions.

bookkeeper

The person who keeps the books or maintains the records of financial transactions. A bookkeeper needs less education or training than an accountant. Bookkeepers record transactions according to rules established by accountants.

book value

Total assets minus total liabilities. (See also *equity*, *net worth*.) Book value also means the value of an asset as recorded in the company's books or financial reports. Book value is often different from the true value. True value may be more or less than book value. The book value of a share of stock is the company's total book value divided by the total number of shares of stock outstanding.

breakeven point

The amount of revenue from sales that exactly equals the amount of expense. Sales above the breakeven point produce a profit. Sales below the breakeven point produce a loss.

budget
A plan for financial performance. Usually shows projected or planned revenues and expenses.

business
A type of commercial or industrial activity such as the steel business or grocery business. Or, as often used in this book, any enterprise engaged in making, buying, or selling goods or services. Can be an individual enterprise, a partnership, a corporation, an LLC, or another form of organization. Also a company or firm.

capital
Money invested in a business by its owners. (See *equity*.) On the right side of the balance sheet. Capital also refers to the buildings, machinery, and other fixed assets used by a business. Thus, a capital investment is an investment in a factory, machine, or other item with a long-term use. A capital budget is the financial plan for the acquisition of capital assets such as factories or machines.

capitalize
To record an expenditure on the balance sheet as an asset to be amortized over the future. The opposite is to expense. For example, research expenditures can be capitalized or expensed. If they are expensed, they are charged against income when the expenditure occurs. If they are capitalized, the expenditure is charged against income over a period of time usually related to the life of the development or products created by the research.

cash
Money available to spend now. Usually money in the company checking account.

cash flow
The amount of actual cash generated by business operations within a period of time. Cash flow differs from profits shown because the accrual method of accounting is used and because noncash expenses are deducted from profits.

chart of accounts
A listing of all the accounts or categories into which business transactions will be classified and recorded. Each account on the chart

usually has a number. Transactions are coded by this number and can then be recorded, stored, and collected by data processing equipment.

company

A business enterprise. Company most often refers to the legal entity. Business may be used as a synonym for company but may also have other meanings.

contingent liability

A liability not recorded on a company's financial statements but that might become due. If a company is being sued, it has a contingent liability that will become a real liability if the company loses the suit. When evaluating a company, look for contingent liabilities.

corporation

An organization chartered by a state. The owners of a corporation are liable to the corporation's creditors only to the extent of the owners' investment in the corporation. If you buy a share of stock for $25 and the corporation fails, you cannot lose more than the $25. This limitation of liability has made the corporation the dominant form of business organization. Limited liability has made it possible to sell stock to raise money for new ventures.

cost accounting

A system of accounting concerned with assigning a fair share of costs to each unit produced. Cost accounting is used primarily in manufacturing companies. When costs are assigned to units, it is possible to arrive at unit selling prices and profits per unit. Many factors affect cost accounting. Most are beyond the scope of this book. Cost accounting is made complex by costs such as the cost of factory electricity, machine depreciation, and plant supervision, which are difficult to assign to specific units. Many cost accounting systems use the concept of standard cost—the cost that is expected for a unit. Actual costs are compared with standard costs to determine a variance. The variance is analyzed to see if it is caused by changing costs, changing selling prices, more or fewer units against which fixed costs are allocated, and so on. Analyzing the variance from standard cost helps suggest management changes. Get a book on cost accounting if your job requires knowledge of this specialized field.

cost of sales, cost of goods sold

The expense or cost of all items sold during an accounting period. Each sale made has a cost of that sale or a cost of the goods sold. In businesses that sell a few items, the cost of each item can be charged as an expense or cost of sales when that item is sold. In businesses with a great many items flowing through, the cost of sales or cost of goods sold is often computed by this formula: cost of sales = beginning inventory + purchases – ending inventory. Cost of sales is a concept that is both difficult and important. It is discussed in great detail in this book. Cost of sales is affected not only by the cost of the items sold, but also by inventory obsolescence, inventory shrinkage, and FIFO or LIFO. (See these entries in the Glossary.)

CPA

Certified Public Accountant. An accountant who has passed a professional test and is certified as qualified to do accounting and auditing.

credit

An accounting entry on the right side of a balance sheet. Usually an increase in liabilities or capital or a reduction in assets. The opposite is debit. Each credit has a balancing debit. Accountants talk about debits and credits. Others seldom use these terms. Of course, credit has several other meanings in business, such as "You must pay cash; your credit is no good." and "We have credited your account with the refund."

debit

An accounting entry on the left side of a balance sheet. Usually an increase in assets or a reduction in liabilities or capital. The opposite is credit. Each debit has a balancing credit.

debt

Something that is owed. (See *liability*.)

deferred charge

See *prepaid expense*.

deferred income

A liability that comes about when a company is paid in advance for goods or services and is liable to provide the goods or services later. For example, when a magazine subscription is paid in advance, the magazine publisher has income, but it is also liable to provide the subscriber magazines for the life of the subscription. The amount in deferred income is reduced as the magazines (or other goods or services) are delivered. The worth of a business is reduced by the amount of goods or services it is obligated to provide in the future.

depreciation
A method of converting an expenditure into an expense. It is an expense that is supposed to reflect the loss in value of a fixed asset. For example, if a machine will completely wear out after ten years of use, the cost of the machine is charged as an expense over the ten-year life rather than all at once when the machine is purchased. Straight-line depreciation would charge an equal amount each year. A machine costing $1,000 depreciated over ten years by the straight-line method would have $100 charged to expense each year for ten years. Accelerated depreciation charges more to expense in the early years and less in later years. Under one accelerated depreciation formula the first-year charge for the $1,000 machine might be $181.82, the fifth-year charge $109.09, and the tenth-year charge $18.18. The choice of depreciation periods and methods is regulated by accounting standards and the IRS.

discounted cash flow
A system for evaluating investment opportunities. The system discounts or reduces the value of future cash flow because cash received in the future is not as valuable as cash available now. (See *present value*.)

dividend
A payment made to stockholders by a corporation. Usually cash. A dividend is a portion of the profits paid to the owners. It is a return on their investment. Dividends are paid with after-tax dollars. They are not a deductible business expense (as loan interest is, for example).

division
A portion of a company, usually operating more or less as a separate entity. Legally, a division is part of the parent company. A subsidiary is a separate legal entity owned by the parent company.

double entry
A system of accounting supposedly devised by an Italian monk in late medieval times. The system requires that every accounting transaction be recorded twice—as a debit and as a credit.

earnings
Net profit after taxes. (See *profit*.)

Earnings per share are the company's total earnings for the accounting period divided by the average number of shares of stock outstanding.

ebitda
Income or earnings before interest, taxes, depreciation, and amortization. Often used as a measure of division, subsidiary, or company performance or value.

equity
The owners' share of a business. Can be computed by subtracting liabilities from assets. (See also *capital, net worth*.)

expenditure
Made when something is acquired for a business—an asset is purchased, salaries are paid, and so on. An expenditure affects the balance sheet. It does not necessarily show up on the income statement or affect the profits at the time the expenditure is made. However, all expenditures eventually show up as expenses, which do affect the income statement and profits. Most expenditures involve the exchange of cash for something. Expenses need not involve cash. (See *expense*.)

expense
(noun) An expenditure chargeable against revenue during an accounting period. An expense results in the reduction of an asset. Not all expenditures are expenses. For example, suppose a company buys a truck. It trades one asset—cash—to acquire another asset. An expenditure has been made, but no expense is recorded. As the truck is used and depreciates, an expense is incurred. This concept of expense is one reason why financial reports do not show numbers that represent spendable cash. (See *expenditure*.) The distinction between expenditure and expense is important in understanding accounting. Expenditures occur when money (or something else of value) changes hands. Expenses occur whenever the expenditure is recorded so as to affect a company's profits. This is often at a different time than the

expenditure. The expense of salaries is recorded before the expenditure of money for salaries is made. The expense of a machine purchase is recorded after the expenditure of money for the machine is made.

(verb) To charge an expenditure against income when the expenditure is incurred. The opposite is to capitalize. Expenditures in areas such as research may be expensed or capitalized. (See *capitalize*.)

FASB
Financial Accounting Standards Board. Creates and maintains standards for accounting. These standards become part of GAAP. (See *GAAP*.)

FIFO, LIFO
Stand for "first in, first out" and "last in, first out"—two methods of determining the cost of sales. Think of the inventory as a stack of goods. Each time new inventory is purchased, it goes on top of the stack. The oldest inventory is on the bottom of the stack. When a sale is made, an item can be taken from the top or bottom of the stack. Taking from the bottom is FIFO. Taking from the top is LIFO. If the item sold is the last one put into the inventory stack, its cost is the latest cost. If the item sold is at the bottom of the stack, its cost is the oldest cost. This is very important in times of rapid inflation or deflation. In inflation, the last item in the stack costs much more than the first item. Under FIFO the cost is lower than under LIFO. A lower cost means higher profit—and more taxes to be paid. In a period of deflation, just the opposite occurs. Unfortunately, the IRS does not permit companies to switch between FIFO and LIFO.

fiscal year
An annual accounting period that does not begin on January 1 and end on December 31. The federal fiscal year runs from October 1 through September 30. Many other fiscal years run from July 1 through June 30. A company can choose its fiscal year.

fixed asset
See *asset*.

fixed cost
A cost or expense that does not change as sales volume changes (in the short run). Fixed costs normally include such items as rent, depreciation, interest, and any salaries unaffected by ups and downs in sales.

Of course, fixed costs are fixed only for the short run. (Leases can be canceled and executives fired.) Extreme shifts in sales volume cause many fixed costs to become unfixed. Fixed costs are a factor in determining breakeven. (See *variable cost*.)

GAAP

Generally Accepted Accounting Principles. These establish consistent ways of accounting for various transactions. GAAP has a great many rules. These have been agreed on by accountants and CPAs and set by FASB.

general and administrative expenses (G&A)

Expenses not attributable to specific business areas such as manufacturing, purchasing, or sales. The president's salary, franchise taxes, executive office rent, and the company switchboard are examples of expenses normally included in G&A.

goodwill

In accounting usage, goodwill is the difference between what a company pays when it buys the assets of another company and the book value of those assets. For example, suppose Company A buys Company B for $1,000,000. Company B has assets with a book value of $800,000. Company A adds these assets to its books. It must also account for the extra $200,000 it paid. Company A does this by entering in its assets the item "Goodwill—$200,000." Of course, real goodwill exists—a company's good reputation, the favor of its customers, and so on. But in accounting, goodwill represents the amount paid in excess of the book value of the assets acquired. Goodwill can be amortized on a straight-line basis over 15 years. Companies search hard for ways to minimize the amount of goodwill they purchase.

income

See *profit*.

income tax

A tax levied by federal, state, or local governments on a company's profits or income. The tax is usually a percentage of the profits before taxes. What is left after income taxes is net profits after taxes.

inflation

An increase in prices or reduction in the value of money that has a major effect on companies and their financial reports. Because assets are shown at original cost, they do not reflect inflated value or the inflated cost of replacing them. Inflation of selling prices can result in increased dollar sales with reduced unit sales, and possibly reduced market share. Sales must go up faster than inflation if a company is to move ahead. Inflation distorts all financial reports. It also results in extra taxes being paid on the inflated income, which drains cash needed to pay for the higher costs. Inflation corrodes all business. Its effects can be insidious.

interest
A charge made or rent paid for the use of money. The interest rate normally is expressed as a percentage of the loan to be paid for one year's use of the money. Interest paid by a company is considered a non operating expense. Interest is nonoperating income when a company earns it, unless the company's principal business is lending money.

inventory
The supply or stock of goods and products that a company has for sale. A manufacturer normally has three kinds of inventory: raw materials waiting to be converted into goods, work in process, and finished goods ready for sale. Inventory is a current asset.

inventory obsolescence
That amount of inventory that is no longer salable. Inventory obsolescence comes about from having more inventory on hand than can be sold. The inventory may be obsolete—old-fashioned or out of style. Or competition may have killed sales. Or too many products may have been manufactured or purchased. The true value of a company's inventory is seldom exactly what is shown on the balance sheet. Often unrecognized inventory obsolescence exists.

inventory shrinkage
A reduction in the amount of inventory that is not easily explainable. The most common cause of shrinkage is probably theft. Other causes include loss, damage by water, insects, and fire.

inventory turnover
A ratio that indicates the amount of inventory a company needs to support a given level of sales. The formula is inventory turnover = cost of sales ÷ average inventory. Retail businesses have a high

inventory turnover—five, ten, or more times a year. This means that they can produce a lot of sales with a small investment in inventory. The turnover number by itself is not too significant. Comparisons with the turnover of similar companies or with the turnover in previous years are more meaningful. If turnover goes down when sales stay up, this may signal that some parts of inventory are becoming obsolete. (Typically, a small portion of any inventory generates a large portion of the sales. A few items turn over rapidly, and others languish. (See *80/20 rule*.)

invested capital
The total of a company's long-term debt and equity. (See *return on investment*.)

journal
A chronological record of business transactions. Journal entries are usually transferred to the ledger.

leasehold improvement
Amounts spent for permanent improvements to rented facilities, such as new walls and lighting. These are fixed assets depreciated over the life of the lease.

ledger
A record of business transactions kept by account.

liability
An amount owed by a company to someone else.

Current liabilities are due within one year or less. Current liabilities usually include accounts payable, accruals such as salaries earned by employees but not yet paid to them, loans due to be paid in a year or less, taxes owed and not yet paid, and so on.

Long-term liabilities normally include mortgages, bonds, and long-term loans. The portion of a long-term liability due within a year is usually included in current liabilities (such as the payments due this year on a mortgage).

liquid
Having lots of cash or assets easily converted to cash. Lenders are usually concerned about a company's liquidity.

long term, long run

These phrases always mean longer than one year. Sometimes they mean far enough in the future so that current conditions can be significantly changed (a new product developed, a new plant constructed, and so on).

loss

The opposite of profit. An excess of expenses over revenues. A loss does not necessarily represent a reduction in cash during the accounting period. But eventually, a loss will be reflected in a reduction in cash.

marginal cost, marginal revenue

Marginal cost is the additional, extra cost incurred by adding one more item. For example, if a plant makes 1,000 widgets a day, what will be the additional cost to make widget number 1,001? This is the marginal cost. Marginal revenue is the additional revenue coming in from selling one more item. According to economic theory, maximum profit comes at the point where marginal revenue exactly equals marginal cost. In practice, this is hard to hit. These concepts are used to consider whether to increase volume.

market

(noun) A group of customers to whom you sell or try to sell products or services.

(verb) To determine customer needs or wants, create products or services to fill those needs or wants, sell to customers, and then distribute the resulting orders. Marketing is a total function, from identification to satisfaction of a customer need or want.

market share

A company's sales as a percentage of the total industry sales to a market. If the total widget sales are 10 million a year, and Acme Widget sells 1 million a year, its market share is 10 percent. A high market share is an opportunity to achieve high profits (unless the high market share comes from excessive price cutting or excessive selling expense). Companies' financial reports would be more useful if they showed market share for principal areas of business.

mortgage

A long-term liability or debt that is secured by specific property. Buildings and machines are often mortgaged. Most other debt is guaranteed by the borrower's general reputation and credit, not by pledging specific assets.

net worth

Total assets minus total liabilities. Net worth is the owner's equity, capital, or stock plus retained earnings. Several terms mean the same thing. Net worth is not necessarily a company's true value.

obsolescence

A reduction in the value of an asset caused by technological change, competition, altered business conditions, style changes, and so on. Machines can become obsolete long before they wear out (buggy whip machines, for example). Inventory becomes obsolete too, as newer models appear or customer tastes change. Obsolescence is recognized by a write-off or write-down of the asset's value. This write-off or write-down (reduction in value) is an expense of the business when it is made. Obsolescence can be a significant expense in high-fashion or high-technology businesses. A major problem in evaluating a business is determining how much obsolescence has not been recognized. Assets often are not as valuable as they appear on the books. Obsolescence is a major reason.

opportunity cost

A useful concept in evaluating alternatives. For instance, if you choose alternative A, you cannot choose B, C, or D. What is the cost or the loss in potential profits of not choosing B, C, or D? This cost or loss of potential profits is the opportunity cost of alternative A. For example, suppose you decide to buy an automobile instead of taking a European vacation. The opportunity cost of buying an automobile is the loss of the vacation's benefits. Too often, we look at the costs of similar items. We compare one automobile to another. Shall we buy a Ford or a Chevy? We ignore the other things we could buy or do if we didn't buy the automobile. We ignore the opportunity cost.

overhead

A cost that does not vary with the level of production or sales. Usually this is a cost not involved in production or sales. Rent usually is considered overhead. The chief executive's salary typically is overhead, too. Overhead costs are difficult to allocate or apportion to any specific unit of sales or production. Fixed costs include overhead but may also include costs involved with production or sales that do not vary with volume. (See *G&A*.)

partnership

A business in which two or more partners (persons, other partnerships, or corporations) pool their resources and share the profits. The partners are liable for partnership debts to the full extent of their assets. (Owners of corporations are liable only to the extent of their equity.) A limited partnership is a special form in which some partners' liability is limited to the amount of their contribution to the partnership, while all the assets of the general partner(s) are subject to claims by creditors. A limited liability company (LLC) is yet another business form that offers limited liability for owners but is taxed like a partnership.

post

To enter business transactions into a journal, ledger, or other financial record.

prepaid expense, deferred charge

An asset already paid for that is being used up or will expire. Insurance paid for in advance is a common example. The insurance protection is an asset. It is paid for in advance, lasts for a period of time, and expires on a fixed date. Travel advances are another common example of prepaid expenses.

present value

A concept that compares the value of money available in the future with the value of money in hand today. The present value of money is compared to the future value. For example, $100 in hand today is worth more than $100 to be available in five years. This is because the $100 in hand today can be invested and earn money. If it is invested at 5 percent, the $100 will grow to $127.63 in five years. To put it another way, $78.35 invested at 5 percent for five years will grow to $100. Thus, the present value of $100 received five years in the future is $78.35. The concept of present value is used to analyze investment opportunities that have a future payoff. All the investment and all the return can be computed at present value to see if the percentage rate of return on the investment is acceptable. Present value is discussed in more detail in Chapter 7.

price-earnings (p/e) ratio

The market price of a share of stock divided by the company's earnings (profit) per share. A company whose stock is selling at $48 a share and whose current earnings for the year are $6 per share has a price-earnings ratio of 8. In periods of great speculation, p/e ratios of hot companies may go as high as 50, 100, 200, or more. $6 per share earnings would have a market price of $300, $600, $1,200, or more. In a depressed economy or for dull companies in static industries, the p/e may be 3 or 4. In periods of speculation, companies try many tricks to boost the p/e ratios so that their highly valued stock can be used in acquisitions or sold at a high price. Price-earnings ratio is a poor method of evaluating a company's real worth.

productivity

The amount of output per unit of labor, capital, and so on. Increasing productivity is a critical function of management. How can each sales representative sell more? How can each machine produce more? How can each file clerk file more? How can each dollar invested in a company produce more profit? Measures of productivity are valuable additions to financial reports.

profit

The amount left over when expenses are subtracted from revenues.

Gross profit is the profit left when cost of sales is subtracted from sales. Gross profit is before any operating expenses are subtracted.

Operating profit is the profit from the primary operations of a business. It is sales or revenues minus cost of sales and minus operating expenses. Operating profit is before nonoperating income and expense and before income taxes.

Net profit before taxes is the operating profit minus nonoperating expenses and plus nonoperating income.

Net profit after taxes is the bottom line. It is the final profit after everything has been subtracted. It is also called income, net income, or earnings. Net profit after taxes is not the same as cash flow and does not represent spendable dollars.

retained earnings

Profits not distributed to stockholders as dividends. Retained earnings are the accumulation of a company's profits less any dividends paid out. Retained earnings usually are not cash. They are normally invested in the company's various assets.

return

A basic component in measuring business performance. Return is defined in different ways but most often is net profit after taxes.

return on investment (ROI)

A measure of the effectiveness and efficiency with which managers use the resources available to them in the business.

return on assets used (ROAU): Usually the operating profit divided by the assets used to produce the profit. This method of computing ROI typically is used for divisions of a company that have no control over liabilities or use of cash. Those are handled by the parent corporation or headquarters.

return on equity (ROE): Usually net profit after taxes divided by the owner's equity, translated into a percentage. A recent survey showed average return on equity (year-end) to be about 12 percent. (But all ROI figures vary by industry.)

return on invested capital (ROIC): Usually net profit after taxes plus interest paid on long-term debt divided by owner's equity plus long-term debt. The investment in this formula is both equity and long-term debt. The return is both profit and interest that is a return on the long-term debt investment. A recent survey showed average return on invested capital to be about 9 percent.

ROI measures are extremely useful in evaluating company performance. But ROI can be used only to compare consistent entities—similar companies in the same industry, or the same company over a period of time. Different companies may have different historic ROIs. Different industries usually have different ROIs. The minimum acceptable ROI must be greater than that which can be realized on a safer investment. If an investor can earn a return of 5 percent from very safe bonds or securities, he will certainly expect a manager to produce better than 5 percent if the investment is made in a business venture with more risk.

revenue
The amounts received by or due a company for the goods or services it provides to customers. Receipts are the cash amounts received. Revenues include receipts as well as amounts still owed to the company for the sales of goods or services. (See *sales*.)

risk
The possibility of loss; inherent in all business activities. Related to return. Low risk is satisfied with low return. High risk requires high return. Risk is difficult to measure, but all business decisions need to take into account the amount of risk involved.

rounding off
Many accountants present financial reports that show numbers to the penny. This is unnecessary and often confuses analysis. As a manager, I have found that financial reports and budgets rounded off to the nearest thousand dollars are satisfactory. The company's size usually determines where to round off.

sales
The amounts received or due a company for goods or services sold to customers. (See *revenue*.)

Gross sales are the total sales before any returns or adjustments.

Net sales are gross sales minus any returns or adjustments made during the accounting period. Sales usually do not include sales taxes or transportation. Unless it is a business that sells for cash, sales don't represent cash. Cash comes in later, when the customer pays the bill. A company cannot live without sales.

short run, short term
A period of time too short to allow significant changes in operations. Usually defined as a year or less.

stock
A certificate that indicates ownership of a portion of a corporation. A share of stock.

Preferred stock promises its owners a dividend that usually is fixed in amount or percentage. Preferred stockholders have preference. They get paid first if there are any profits.

Common stock has no preference and no fixed rate of return. It is the most common kind of stock.

Treasury stock is originally issued to stockholders but is returned to the corporation by purchase or as a gift.

Authorized but unissued stock. The number of shares of stock a company can have usually is set by its charter or by official corporate action. If a corporation is authorized to have one million shares, and it sells 750,000, it has 250,000 authorized but unissued shares. These may be sold later or used to acquire another company.

stock or goods
Refers to the inventory (stock on hand) available for sale. The stockroom is where inventory is kept. Overstocked means that too much inventory is on hand.

subsidiary
A company owned or controlled by another company. A subsidiary is a separate legal entity. A division is not.

sunk costs
Money already spent and gone. It cannot be recovered no matter what course of action is followed. In comparing alternative courses of action, it is usually wise to forget about sunk costs. Bad decisions are made when managers pretend they can somehow recoup sunk costs.

surplus
See *retained earnings*.

tax
An amount paid to a government body.

Income tax is a portion or percentage of the net profit before taxes.

Franchise tax is a tax paid on the right to do business. It may be a flat sum or be related to something like the amount of original capital. It is not related to profits.

Property tax is a tax levied on the value of a company's property or assets.

Sales tax is a tax collected by business as a percentage of the sales price and then sent to the taxing government. The business acts as the tax collector.

The kinds of taxes are many and are limited only by the ingenuity of government bodies. Taxes have a major impact on business results. As a general principle, don't make any decision for tax reasons that would not be a good decision without tax considerations.

trial balance

At the close of an accounting period, the transactions posted in the ledger are added up—those that affect assets and those that affect liabilities and capital. A test or trial balance sheet is prepared, with assets on one side and liabilities and capital on the other. The two sides should balance. If they don't, the accountants must search through the transactions to find the reason why. They must make the balance sheet balance.

variable cost

A cost that changes as sales or production change. If a business is producing nothing and selling nothing, the variable cost should be zero. Fixed costs will continue regardless of production or sales levels.

working capital

Current assets minus current liabilities. In most businesses the major components of working capital are cash, accounts receivable, and inventory minus accounts payable. As a business grows, it has more accounts receivable and needs more inventory. Thus, its need for working capital increases. Increases in working capital can come from retained earnings, borrowing, or selling more stock.

write-down

The partial reduction in an asset's value, recognizing obsolescence or other losses in the asset's value. (See *obsolescence*.)

write-off

The complete reduction in an asset's value, recognizing that the asset no longer has any value.

3

The Balance Sheet

The first financial report we cover in this book is the balance sheet. The balance sheet shows a business's financial position at a specific time. It is a snapshot of a business, not a record of its performance over a period of time. The balance sheet pinpoints financial status at the close of business at the end of an accounting period.

The Balance Sheet Balances

The balance sheet has two sides. The numbers on each side must add up to the same total. The balance sheet balances.

On one side of the balance sheet are assets (things of value the company owns). On the other side are liabilities (debts the company owes) and capital (the owners' share of the company). The balance sheet is described by this equation:

$$\text{assets} = \text{liabilities} + \text{capital}$$

Every entry into or out of one part of the balance sheet must be balanced by a corresponding entry in another part of the balance sheet. This is so that the bottom totals will remain in balance. This is basic double-entry bookkeeping.

Words alone are not enough to convey the full meaning of all this. So we will construct a balance sheet of our own. Before we do, Figures 3.1 and 3.2 illustrate typical corporate balance sheets. If you have looked at any company financial reports, you have probably seen examples of balance sheets. Look at the following figures. Do they follow the equation (assets = liabilities + capital)? Do they balance?

Figure 3.1 Company A Balance Sheet

Assets	Current Year	Previous Year
	July 31	
Cash	$75,986	$72,002
Accounts receivable	89,793	99,502
Inventory		
Materials and supplies	138,995	176,295
Work in process	33,978	23,155
	172,973	199,450
Prepaid expenses	8,176	5,639
Total current assets	346,928	376,593
Property, plant, and equipment—at cost		
Land	56,460	56,460
Buildings and production lines	722,776	660,001
Shop machinery and equipment	175,090	157,774
Office furniture, fixtures, and equipment	34,521	34,497
Autos and trucks	76,722	68,439
	1,065,569	977,171
Less accumulated depreciation	319,124	266,814
	746,445	710,357
Other assets	233	4,233
Total assets	$1,093,606	$1,091,183
Liabilities		
Current liabilities		
Accounts payable	$60,861	$22,803
Current maturities of long-term debt	53,939	41,218
Accrued liabilities		
Federal income tax	0	19,071
Other accruals	13,160	12,890

Liabilities	Current Year	Previous Year
Other current liabilities	0	9,000
Total current liabilities	127,960	104,982
Long-term debt	585,834	605,742
Less current maturities	53,939	41,218
	531,895	564,524
Total liabilities	659,855	669,506
Stockholders' Equity		
Common stock: 1,000,000 shares of $1.00 par value authorized, 322,129 shares issued and outstanding; 10,000 shares of $100.00 par value authorized, 713 shares issued and outstanding	322,129	71,300
Additional paid-in capital	27,871	64,442
Retained earnings	83,751	285,935
Total stockholders' equity	433,751	421,677
Total liabilities and stockholders' equity	$1,093,606	1,091,183

Figure 3.2 Company B Balance Sheet: Consolidated Balance Sheet as of December 31 (All Figures in Thousands)

Assets	Current Year	Previous Year
Current assets:		
Cash and time deposits	$3,694	$1,230
Short-term investments, at cost that approximates market	300	350
Accounts receivable, less allowance for doubtful accounts, $252,636 in current year and $201,230 in previous year	9,769	7,456
Inventories:		
Finished goods	5,073	3,432
Work in process	1,528	1,173
Raw materials	5,193	4,320
Total inventories	11,794	8,925
Prepaid expenses	98	103
Total current assets	25,655	18,064
Property, plant, and equipment:		
Land	594	482
Building and building improvements	4,110	3,765
Machinery and equipment	12,801	10,701
Furniture and fixtures	806	687
Construction in progress	676	0
Total	18,987	15,635
Less accumulated depreciation	6,493	4,865
Property, plant, and equipment—net	12,494	10,770
Other assets:	570	415
Total	$38,719	$29,249

Liabilities and Shareholders' Equity	Current Year	Previous Year
Current liabilities:		
Accounts payable	$2,810	$1,753
Federal, state, and foreign taxes payable	2,614	798
Current maturities of long-term debt	59	59
Accrued payroll and other compensation	1,553	975
Other accrued expenses	1,015	371
Total current liabilities	8,051	3,956
Long-term debt	139	199
Deferred income taxes	1,176	982
Total liabilities	9,366	5,137
Shareholders' equity:		
Common stock: authorized, 7,000,000 shares of $.10 par value; issued and outstanding, 3,578,913 shares	357	357
Paid-in capital	1,145	1,145
Retained earnings	27,851	22,610
Shareholders' equity	29,353	24,112
Total	$38,719	$29,249

Does this balance sheet balance? Assets = liabilities = capital.

Acme Widget Company

To construct our own balance sheet, we need a company. Let's start one. We will call it Acme Widget Company. We will buy a widget-making machine, purchase raw materials, and produce a lot of widgets. We will sell the widgets to widget users and make a lot of money, which we will share generously with the tax collector.

You and I will each put up $40,000. In exchange for this money, we will get shares of stock in the Acme Widget Company. Figure 3.3 shows how this is recorded on the Acme Widget balance sheet.

Figure 3.3 Acme Widget Company Balance Sheet 1

Assets		Liabilities and Capital	
Cash	$80,000	Liabilities	$0
		Capital	
		Common Stock	80,000
Total Assets	$80,000	Total Liabilities and Capital	$80,000

On the asset side we record the $80,000 we put into the Acme Widget bank account as cash. On the liabilities and capital side we record the value of the stock certificates we were issued.

We need more money to get Acme Widget started. So we visit our friendly bank and borrow $60,000 for Acme Widget on a six-month loan. Figure 3.4 shows how our balance sheet looks after we get the loan.

Figure 3.4 Acme Widget Company Balance Sheet 2

Assets		Liabilities and Capital	
Cash	$140,000	Liabilities	
		Note Payable	$60,000
		Capital	
		Common Stock	80,000
Total Assets	$140,000	Total Liabilities and Capital	$140,000

In Figure 3.4, as in Figure 3.3, you can see that the transaction is recorded on both sides of the balance sheet and that the bottom totals are the same. They balance.

Now we will buy a $48,000 widget-making machine. We will also buy $20,000 worth of raw materials to make widgets on the machine. We have acquired the machine and the raw materials, but we have not yet paid for them. These bills will be due in 30 days.

We have also leased factory space. We paid a month's rent in advance—$1,000.

These transactions are recorded on the balance sheet, as shown in Figure 3.5.

Figure 3.5 Acme Widget Company Balance Sheet 3

Assets		Liabilities and Capital	
Cash	$139,000	Liabilities	
Inventory	20,000	Accounts Payable	$68,000
Prepaid Expenses	1,000	Note Payable	60,000
Fixed Assets	48,000	Total Liabilities	$128,000
		Capital	
		Common Stock	80,000
Total Assets	$208,000	Total Liabilities and Capital	$208,000

Let's look at each item in Figure 3.5. Our cash is still all there, except for the $1,000 we paid in advance rent. We have acquired an inventory of raw materials—$20,000 worth. The rent is a prepaid expense (see the Glossary in Chapter 2) and is recorded at $1,000. The widget machine is a fixed asset. (Again, see the Glossary. As we use these various accounting terms, it is a good idea to go back to the Glossary to be sure you have an idea of what they mean.) We paid $48,000 for the machine, so that is its value as an asset at this time.

Now look at the liabilities. Accounts payable of $68,000 represents the $48,000 we owe to the widget machine supplier plus the $20,000 we owe to the raw materials supplier.

The note payable is the amount we borrowed from the bank.

Capital still shows our stock ownership of $80,000—our initial investment in Acme Widget.

Total assets are equal to total liabilities and capital. The balance sheet continues to balance as we enter items in two places. For example, we put the value of the widget machine on the asset side and the amount we owed on it on the liability side. In the case of the rent payment, we added it to the assets as a prepaid expense but also subtracted it from our cash asset.

Each transaction during the course of the Acme Widget operations will be similarly recorded in two places so that the balance sheet always stays in balance. These transactions are usually not recorded directly on the balance sheet. They go into journals (chronological records of transactions) and into ledgers (records of transactions by area or account, such as cash or accounts payable). At the end of an accounting period, the information recorded in the journals and ledgers is transferred to a balance sheet for the end of that period.

Accountants and other people use worksheets in preparing financial reports. It is time for you to learn how to prepare your own worksheet. Then you will go from that to preparing a balance sheet.

Acme Widget's Year-End Balance Sheet

Acme Widget's operations during the year will affect a number of accounts. The balance sheet needs a number of headings to reflect the transactions. The following are the headings or accounts you will use on your worksheet:

Assets

- *Cash*. Cash available in the bank, or elsewhere, to spend.
- *Accounts receivable*. Amounts owed to Acme by its customers.
- *Inventory*
  - ➤ *Raw materials*. The stock of raw materials waiting to be made into widgets.
  - ➤ *Finished goods*. The stock of completed widgets ready to sell.
- *Prepaid expenses*. A payment made in advance—in this case, rent.
- *Fixed assets*. Machinery, equipment, buildings, and so on used over a long period of time in the business—in this case, the widget machine.
  - ➤ *Depreciation*. The portion of the original cost of the fixed assets used up or expensed since purchase.

Liabilities

- *Accounts payable*. Amounts owed by Acme to its suppliers.
- *Notes payable*. Amounts owed by Acme to the bank or other lenders; due within a year or less.
  - ➤ *Accruals*. Salaries and taxes owed by Acme but not yet paid.

Capital

- *Common stock*. The amount put in by investors to buy Acme's common stock.
- *Retained earnings*. Acme's net profits after taxes, less any dividends paid to stockholders. In terms of the worksheet, you will see that items that do not affect other assets or liabilities do affect retained earnings by increasing or decreasing profits.

If you need further help on these terms, see the Glossary.

During its first year, Acme Widget has the following transactions:

1. Investors purchase $80,000 of common stock.

   We saw this on the balance sheet in Figure 3.3. On a worksheet it might look like this:

   $80,000 stock sale to investors: ⊦ $80,000 cash / + $80,000 common stock.

This worksheet entry shows that this transaction adds $80,000 to cash assets. It balances this by adding $80,000 to common stock capital. The slash separates the two balancing entries.

Take a piece of paper. 8 1/2×11 will be fine. Put a label at the top. It should show that this is the worksheet for the Acme Widget balance sheet at the end of the first year.

After you have labeled your worksheet, put in entry 1, just shown. When you have finished, go on to entry 2, shown next. There will be 18 transactions for Acme Widget's first year of operation. For the early ones, I will give you the entry I would put on the worksheet. For the later transactions you will make your own entries.

After you have completed your worksheet, you will proceed to make up a balance sheet for Acme Widget Company. This kind of hands-on experience will be much more useful than just reading about balance sheets. So get your worksheet paper ready.

2. Acme borrows $60,000 from the bank on a six-month note or loan (see Figure 3.4). The worksheet might look like this:

   Borrow $60,000: + $60,000 cash / + $60,000 notes payable

3. Acme buys a $48,000 widget machine. Owes the machine supplier.

   + $48,000 fixed assets / + $48,000 accounts payable

4. Acme buys $20,000 of raw materials. Owes the supplier.

+ $20,000 inventory – raw materials / + $20,000 accounts payable

5. Acme rents space. Pays $1,000 for one month's rent in advance.

– $1,000 cash / + $1,000 prepaid expenses

In this transaction the entries affect only the asset side of the balance sheet. Therefore, the worksheet must show a plus (+) and a minus (–) to maintain balance. (Transactions 3, 4, and 5 are shown in Figure 3.5.)

6. The bank's note is repaid at the end of the six months. The worksheet might look like this:

Repay bank loan.

– $60,000 cash / – $60,000 notes payable (We'll ignore the interest on the loan.)

7. The machine is paid for.

– $48,000 cash / – $48,000 accounts payable

8. The raw materials are paid for.

– $20,000 cash / – $20,000 accounts payable

9. Raw materials for 40,000 more widgets are purchased. The raw materials cost $4.00 for each widget that can be made from them. When the year ends, we have not paid the supplier for the last order for raw materials for 10,000 widgets. The worksheet might look like this:

Purchase $160,000 raw materials; pay for $120,000.

+ $160,000 inventory—raw materials / – $120,000 cash / + $40,000 accounts payable

This series of transactions requires more than one entry to arrive at a balance. This will often be true. Be sure that each part of a worksheet transaction balances by itself.

10. Enough raw materials for 41,000 widgets are manufactured into finished widgets ($164,000 worth).

+ $164,000 inventory—finished goods / – $164,000 inventory—raw materials

11. Acme sells 36,500 widgets at $8.00 each. During the year, customers pay for 28,000 widgets. At year-end Acme is still owed for 8,500 widgets.

There are really several transactions here. Let's look at each one. The first is a transaction affecting inventory:

36,500 widgets sold: – $146,000 inventory—finished goods / ...

How do we balance this one? When we take the widgets out of inventory and ship them to customers, we have reduced the inventory asset by $146,000. Have we increased any other asset by a like amount? No, we have not. This transaction does not balance by increasing an asset.

Have we reduced any liability by $146,000 to balance the reduction in the asset? No. Nothing like that has occurred.

Let's look at capital. Shipping 36,500 widgets doesn't affect common stock. But the shipment does affect retained earnings. When we ship 36,500 widgets, inventory is reduced by $146,000. Retained earnings are reduced by the same amount. The balance sheet continues to balance.

The shipment is a result of sales. The sales are for $292,000. The amount of $292,000 goes into accounts receivable, because the customers owe us this amount for the shipment. We have increased the accounts receivable asset by $292,000. What balances this entry?

Did any other asset go down by this amount? No. Do we owe someone more money (did we add to our liabilities) as a result of this sale? No.

So again we look to capital—specifically, to retained earnings: sales of $292,000: + $292,000 accounts receivable / + $292,000 retained earnings

The next transaction occurs when customers pay for 28,000 of the 36,500 widgets. This results in + $224,000 cash / – $224,000 accounts receivable.

Note that we ended up with a profit shown in retained earnings of $146,000, *even though* we collected no cash. When the cash was collected, it did not affect profits or retained earnings. Profits and retained earnings are not the same as cash.

12. We must depreciate the widget machine. We have determined that the expenditure for its purchase can be expensed (written off) over ten years. At the end of ten years its value on our books will be zero. Its original cost of $48,000 will be reduced to zero whether or not the machine is still useful. We decide to depreciate the widget machine on a straight-line basis over ten years. This means that the depreciation will be the same for each month of the ten years. The monthly depreciation will be the original cost, $48,000, divided by the number of months of useful life, 120. So the monthly depreciation is $400, and $4,800 for the year. This is entered into the worksheet as follows:

– $4,800 depreciation of fixed assets / – $4,800 retained earnings

Again, we have an entry that is balanced by an effect on profits and retained earnings. We have paid out the cash already. *When* the cash was paid to buy the machine did not directly affect retained earnings. This was an expenditure, but it was not yet an expense. It is expenses that affect profits and retained earnings. Depreciation is an expense, but the purchase of the fixed asset is not. It is an expenditure.

Depreciation is one of the more difficult accounting concepts. It is a means of charging the cost of a fixed asset such as a machine or a building to expense as the machine or building is being used. The expense is charged over the useful life of the asset. The IRS and experience set guidelines for what the useful life is. We know that a building usually lasts longer than a car. Buildings are usually depreciated over 20 to 40 years, and cars over three or four years. (Of course, buildings can have useful lives of hundreds of years. Cars can last for ten or 20 years. But extreme cases are not the basis for depreciation.)

Depreciation can be straight-line—the same amount of depreciation expense each period. Or it can be accelerated, with a greater depreciation expense in the early years of the asset's life, and less later. In any case, depreciation cannot add up to more than the original cost. Some people view depreciation as a means of accumulating the money to buy a replacement for the machine, building, or whatever is being depreciated. This is not the purpose. Depreciation serves to change an expenditure, which does not affect profits and retained earnings, into an expense, which does. It is a means of getting the cost of a fixed asset off the balance sheet over a period of time as the asset is used.

Sales increase profits. Depreciation reduces profits and thereby reduces retained earnings on the balance sheet. Let's go on.

13. Acme rents space for $1,000 per month. Each month's rent is paid in advance. Transaction 5 recorded the payment of the first month's rent. This rent was recorded as a prepaid expense. It was used up when Acme occupied the space for the month. Put this on your worksheet.

14. During the year, Acme pays rent each month. It makes 12 payments in addition to the one just discussed. Put these 12 rent payments on your worksheet. These payments affect three items on the balance sheet.

15. As owner-managers of Acme, you and I deserve a salary. Let's pay ourselves $4,000 a month each. We will get our salaries five days after the close of the month in which they are earned. Put this on your worksheet. It affects three items. (To keep it simple, we'll ignore all the payroll taxes.)

16. Acme has postage, telephone, and other office expenses. They total $200 a month and are paid during the month. Put this on your worksheet.

17. Acme spends $8,000 to print an advertising circular promoting its widgets. An additional $2,000 is spent to mail the circular to prospective widget customers.

18. Acme owes $3,120 in income taxes on its profits from first-year operations. It won't have to pay these taxes until several months after year-end. When you put this on your worksheet, you have finished all the transactions. (We consider only federal income taxes, ignoring all other state and local taxes.)

A "Trial Balance"

You should now have all 18 transactions recorded on your worksheet. Using these transactions, we will construct a balance sheet showing the financial position of Acme Widget Company at the end of its first year of operations.

It is difficult to go from the worksheet to the balance sheet. An intermediate step is a great help. Take another piece of paper. Also have a calculator. It will speed your computations.

You can use any format that is convenient for you. I find the one shown in Figure 3.6 to be good for me. I go through my worksheet that shows all the entries for transactions 1 through 18. My trial balance worksheet has all the headings used in the worksheet, such as Cash, Accounts Receivable, and so on. Each entry on the worksheet is then put on the trial balance worksheet under its appropriate heading, with a plus or minus sign. For example, the first transaction would be recorded as +$80,000 under Cash and then +$80,000 under Common Stock. Be sure to allow enough room for all the entries you will make under each heading.

Figure 3.6 Acme Widget Company Trial Balance Worksheet

Assets			
Cash	Accounts Receivable	Inventory Raw Materials	Inventory Finished Goods
Prepaid Expenses	Fixed Assets	Depreciation	**Total Assets**

Liabilities			
Accounts Payable	Notes Payable	Accruals	**Total Liabilities**

Capital			
Common Stock	Retained Earnings		**Total Capital**

Make your own trial balance worksheet and fill it in.

Mine shows total assets of $148,800. Total liabilities are $51,120. Total capital is $97,680. (Total liabilities + total capital = $148,800.) What does yours show?

This is a trial balance, so go back and check it if it doesn't balance. (Don't forget: assets = liabilities + capital.)

When you have things in balance—or when you are completely and hopelessly stumped—you can check out the worksheet I have prepared for myself. You can also see the trial balance worksheet I did. These are shown in Appendix A. If we don't agree, check carefully to see where you are making a mistake. Perhaps you didn't subtract depreciation from fixed assets. Or perhaps your calculator needs new batteries.

Constructing the Balance Sheet

With the trial balance worksheet it is easy to construct a balance sheet. Do one on a sheet of paper as shown in Figure 3.7. Use the format shown in Figure 3.3. Add up all the entries under each heading. (Remember, some are plus and some are minus.) The total for each heading will then go on to the balance sheet under that heading.

Figure 3.7 Acme Widget Company Balance Sheet for the First Year of Operations

Assets	Liabilities
Cash	Accounts payable
Accounts receivable	Notes payable
Inventory	Accruals
Raw materials	**Total liabilities**
Finished goods	
Total inventory	**Capital**
Prepaid expenses	Common stock
Fixed assets	Retained earnings
Less depreciation	**Total capital**
Net fixed assets	
Total assets	**Total liabilities and capital**

When you have finished constructing your balance sheet, you can compare it with one that I did. Mine is in Appendix A.

Acme Widget Company doesn't have much cash according to my figures. Is Acme in big trouble? Or is it doing well for a new company? How much would you be willing to pay for Acme at this point?

We will analyze the balance sheet in the next chapter. Try to answer the questions asked in this chapter now. This will help you see what kind of analysis might be needed.

Summary

The balance sheet is a statement of a company's financial position at a moment in time. It shows the assets—all the things of value a company owns—on the left side (or on the top). It shows the liabilities—what a company owes—on the right side (or on the bottom). Also on the right side (or bottom) of the balance sheet is shown capital—the amount invested and the amount earned (or lost) by the company's owners. The total of the assets equals the total of the liabilities and capital. The formula is assets = liabilities + capital.

Principal assets we have covered are cash, accounts receivable, inventory, prepaid expenses, and fixed assets (less depreciation).

Principal liabilities we have covered are accounts payable, notes payable, and accruals. Principal capital items covered are common stock and retained earnings.

A balance sheet shows scores. The cash item is probably real. Normally it can be spent. Other items may or may not be what the numbers show. The accounts receivable may be owed by deadbeats who will never pay. The inventory may be out-of-date and unsalable. The machinery or other fixed assets may be obsolete or falling apart long before their so-called useful life is up.

On the other hand, assets purchased in prior years may be much more valuable today due to inflation. Any balance sheet is an estimate. The estimate can be more or less accurate, depending on many factors.

Whether the estimate is good or bad, the balance sheet must balance. Assets must equal liabilities plus capital. That's how the rules are set up for keeping this score.

4

More Balance Sheet

This chapter continues the discussion of the balance sheet. We will introduce some new concepts and factors. But before we plunge back into the balance sheet itself, we need to cover a few other items.

Cost Versus Value

Items shown on the balance sheet are shown at original cost, unless they have been written down. This means that items go onto the balance sheet at their original cost. If something is purchased at an inflated cost, it goes on the balance sheet at that cost, even if it is actually worth much less.

If an asset is purchased at a great bargain and its value is really much greater than the cost, it still goes onto the balance sheet at its cost.

Assets may be reduced in value—written down—when the company wants to recognize a loss in value. A loss in value may arise when a customer goes bankrupt and can't pay its bills. This customer's account receivable is not worth its original value.

Inventory may be reduced in value when it goes out of style or is replaced by a new model or can't be sold because of tough competition.

A fixed asset can be reduced in value, too. Perhaps it can no longer do the job. A buggy whip machine may operate perfectly to turn out buggy whips. But if there is no longer any demand for that product, the value of a machine making that product may well be greatly reduced. It may be worth nothing but scrap value.

A complete loss of value results in a write-off. A reduction in value results in a write-down. Well-run and honest companies take their write-offs and write-downs as soon as the asset loses value. But some companies try to appear worth more than they really are. They do not take any write-downs or write-offs. Their assets may be shown at values far above their actual worth.

In analyzing any operation, you must look at the asset side of the balance sheet. Consider whether the amounts shown are the true values. Perhaps they are overstated, and write-downs or write-offs should be applied.

As a general rule, any company in serious financial difficulty is overstating the value of its assets. Accounts receivable may be worth 60 percent to 75 percent of what is shown. Inventory may be worth only 10 cents for every dollar shown.

Of course, analysis can show hidden values. For example, a company balance sheet may show its factory and the adjacent land at the original cost of $150,000, less depreciation of the building. Meanwhile, the surrounding area has expanded rapidly. Raw land is selling for $15 per square foot. If the factory were torn down and the land sold, the company could get $1,650,000 for the property. Such a company's balance sheet would be greatly understating the true worth of its assets.

A balance sheet is not exact. It can reveal, and it can hide. It is one of the primary means of keeping score in business, but the scores shown on the balance sheet must be analyzed.

Intangible Assets

Intangible assets are not physical objects or tangible things such as cash or accounts receivable. Patents and copyrights are good examples of intangible assets. Other examples are licenses, franchises, contracts, and other agreements that give a company valuable rights.

These kinds of assets lack the solid material substance of buildings or machines or goods in the warehouse. But they are certainly real. For many companies, intangible assets are the most valuable assets.

The patent that gives a chemical company a monopoly on a valuable chemical may be that company's most valuable asset. Similarly, the copyrights that a publishing company controls give it the rights to best-selling books, which can be the basis of the company's success.

A franchise for an exclusive territory, a license for a process or product, a marketing or distribution agreement, a long-term service contract—these are all valuable intangible assets.

However, often these valuable assets do not appear on the balance sheet. There are sound tax reasons for not putting them on the balance sheet. Often there are other reasons as well. Almost every company has some important intangible assets that are not on the balance sheet.

The employees' know-how and energy is an extremely important asset that is never shown on balance sheets. Of course, it is difficult to put a value on employee capability, but don't ignore it. Just because it is not listed on the balance sheet does not mean that it has no value.

The same is true of other intangible assets. One of my big mistakes was to value a potential acquisition in terms of assets shown on its balance sheet. The company's computer programs and database had cost hundreds of thousands of dollars to develop. They were one of the company's major assets. But they were not shown on the balance sheet. My offer to purchase the company did not allow enough for this intangible but valuable asset that was not recorded. Another company made a better offer and made the acquisition.

When looking at the balance sheet of any company, always ask what assets vital to the company's success are *not* shown on the balance sheet.

It is often wise to prepare a supplement to the balance sheet on which you list the important assets that the accountants have not shown on the balance sheet.

Sometimes the balance sheet shows intangible assets. If it does, be cautious. Putting a value on intangible assets is often very difficult. Who really knows what a patent or franchise is worth? This difficulty in valuation is one reason that accountants often resist including intangible assets on balance sheets. A majority of companies prefer not to show most intangible assets. When a company does show significant intangible assets, my suspicious mind asks whether management is trying to pump up the company's value with hot air.

There are two sides to the intangible asset coin. If a company lists them, they may be inflated. If they are not listed, the company value may be understated.

Goodwill

A special kind of intangible asset is found on many balance sheets—goodwill. This term does not mean the same thing to accountants that it means to the layperson. This goodwill arises from acquisitions.

If Acme Widget were to acquire another company's assets, it would usually pay a price different from the value of those assets shown on the books of the selling company. Acme would pay more or less than the book value. You have seen that the values shown on the balance sheet are not necessarily the "true" values. They are unlikely to be the values on which a buyer and seller would agree.

If Acme paid more for the assets of another company than the book value of those assets, there is a problem. How does Acme account for the payment in excess of the book value? To keep the balance sheet in balance, the payment made must be balanced by the assets acquired. Since the payment is greater than the stated value of the assets, another kind of asset is invented to absorb the extra amount. This is goodwill.

Accountants invented goodwill to represent the excess of purchase price over book value. In some cases it really is goodwill—a company's reputation and its customers' goodwill. Such goodwill makes the other assets more valuable. This kind of goodwill is an intangible but valuable asset.

In other cases, goodwill represents inflation that has not been recognized on the balance sheet. Or it may be the premium paid to buy out a competitor. Goodwill can arise from a number of circumstances. It represents an excess of cost paid over the book value of acquired assets.

Most executives prefer not to have goodwill on their balance sheets. It does not represent anything concrete, and it is an expenditure that cannot be recovered through use. After much wrangling, the tax code was changed to allow goodwill to be amortized. A portion of the goodwill can be charged as an expense over time. Currently goodwill can be amortized on a straight-line basis (the same amount each year) over 15 years.

With many acquisitions, much scrambling occurs to find ways to reduce or eliminate goodwill. The IRS has plugged most palatable ways. So goodwill is often found on companies' balance sheets.

When evaluating a company's worth, it is usually safe to discount or even ignore the goodwill asset. However, the company may well have important hidden assets. Its reputation and its customers' goodwill may be among these. But this is usually different from the goodwill shown on the balance sheet. Goodwill represents another reason to be cautious in interpreting and analyzing balance sheets.

Reserves and Allowances

Most balance sheets show reserves or allowances. These are reductions in the value of assets because of expected problems.

For example, most large companies find that a certain percentage of their customers do not pay their bills. The company may not know how many dollars of uncollected accounts there will be in any given year. But an estimate can be made. From this estimate a reserve for doubtful accounts or an allowance for bad debts can be set up. This reserve or allowance is subtracted from the value of the accounts receivable.

Similarly, large inventories usually have some items that cannot be sold at full price. Perhaps they are out of style or obsolete or were damaged in the warehouse. The company may not know exactly how much the value of the total inventory should be reduced to allow for this. But an estimate can be made. A reserve or allowance for inventory obsolescence can be set up. This reserve or allowance reduces the inventory's value.

These are the two principal reserves or allowances. But any assets can have a reserve or allowance for possible loss in value. Even cash can lose value. Changes in foreign currency exchange rates can cause changes in the value of cash.

Setting up a reserve or allowance reduces an asset's value. The balance sheet must balance. So a corresponding entry must be made somewhere else. Where?

Setting up a reserve or allowance reduces an asset. It also reduces the owner's equity. Retained earnings are reduced to balance the reduction in the asset. Setting up a reserve or allowance creates no debt or obligation to pay someone. It doesn't increase the value of any other asset. So it must reduce retained earnings.

Any business of any size that shows no reserves or allowances may be overvaluing its assets. The amount of reserves or allowances can be subject to bad estimates or just plain fudging. During recessions, many companies find that they do not have enough reserves for bad debts. Rosy predictions of profits can be jolted when reserves have to be adjusted to reflect the actual situation.

The Going Concern Assumption

Almost every financial report you see is based on the assumption that the business will continue indefinitely. The going concern assumption is important. It may be false. If a business is about to go under, its assets will be worth a great deal less than if the business is to continue. A company going out of business finds it difficult to sell its inventory. Sales efforts let down. Production quality controls slip. Certain items are unavailable because depleted inventory won't be replenished. Customers often won't buy an incomplete line. Odd inventory items are salable only at deep discounts or on liberal credit terms.

Shaky customers seldom bother to pay a company they won't be doing business with in the future. Bad debts shoot up.

For these and other reasons, the assets of a company going out of business usually are worth much less than if the company were to continue in business. Almost all financial reports assume that a company plans to stay in business—that it is a going concern.

Estimates Are Everywhere

A great many numbers on financial reports are estimates. They are not exact amounts, even if the numbers show exact pennies. Reserves and allowances are estimates. Intangible assets shown on the balance sheet are surely estimated as to value.

Timing causes estimates to be made. Often the numbers for the last month are estimated because management wants a 12-month report before the final results of the last month can be calculated. So estimates for the 12th month are added to the actual figures for the preceding 11 months.

Many numbers on financial reports are estimates. Some are very close to actual. Some are not so close. Some estimates are made to be as close to the actual as possible. Some estimates are made to conceal the likely truth. There are rosy estimates and gloomy estimates. Each has its purposes.

Always be aware that at least part of any financial report is made up of estimates, not real, actual, "true" figures. Where estimates speed up useful management reports, they can be good. Where they are used to obscure the true situation, they can be bad.

Purpose and Perspective

Accounting serves different purposes. Financial reports are viewed from different perspectives. The balance sheet for the same time for the same company may have different versions.

Reports prepared for tax authorities may be different from reports prepared for shareholders. Reports for tax purposes may seek to minimize profits so as to minimize taxes. Reports for shareholders may try to maximize profits to make the company's stock appear more valuable.

Accountants can treat the same transaction in different ways to arrive at different results. For example, depreciation might be straight-line or accelerated. Footnotes usually tell of the existence of different financial reports or different methods of computing profits and asset values. Whenever they appear, *always* read the footnotes to financial reports.

This is important enough to repeat. Always read the footnotes to financial reports.

If there are two different financial reports for the same company for the same period, which one is the true report?

By now your answer should be, "Neither one; it depends."

There is no such thing as a "true" financial report. Each report is true—insofar as the estimates and assumptions are true, and insofar as it is true to the purpose for which it is intended.

Whether or not a financial report is true for you depends on your perspective. Are you looking at the report as one of the company's managers? As a tax agent? As a potential acquirer? As an investor in the company's stock? As someone considering employment with the company? Each perspective calls for a financial report that may differ from others if a picture most useful to that perspective is to be shown.

If I were to choose one financial report as "true," it is the one that is most conservative and cautious in valuing assets. This is often the report prepared for tax purposes. When looking at a potential acquisition, I always try to examine the tax returns. These numbers can be weighed against numbers shown in other reports.

Purpose and perspective affect the numbers shown on financial reports.

We began this chapter discussing original cost versus value. We went from there to intangible assets with a special look at goodwill. Then reserves and allowances were discussed. The going business assumption was presented. Then we saw that balance sheets and other financial reports contain many estimates and can vary depending on purpose and perspective. The thrust of all these points has been to undermine the idea that there is such a thing as a "true" financial report that completely and accurately reflects the company's status.

Before we get back to the actual balance sheet, we need to present some other concepts.

Current Versus Noncurrent Balance Sheet Items

Most balance sheets are divided into current and noncurrent sections. Current assets include all assets that can be expected to turn into cash within a short period of time—usually a year. Included in current assets are cash, marketable securities, accounts receivable, inventories, and prepaid expenses or deferred charges likely to be used up in a year or less.

Current liabilities normally are those that will be paid off in a short time—a year or less. Included in current liabilities are accounts payable, notes payable within a year, accrued expenses and taxes, and that portion of long-term debt due within the next 12 months—the current installments due.

Noncurrent assets are those not likely to be converted to cash quickly. Fixed assets are the major noncurrent assets. Goodwill and other intangible assets also are noncurrent.

Noncurrent or long-term liabilities include all long-term debt such as bonds, term loans, and mortgages. However, the installments due on this debt within the next 12 months are considered a current liability.

Capital is noncurrent.

Working Capital

Working capital is one of the more commonly used scores. Working capital equals current assets minus current liabilities. Theoretically, working capital is the capital in the business that is working on a day-by-day basis to produce profits.

Look at the first-year balance sheet for Acme Widget. Use your own or the one in Appendix A. Identify and total the current assets. Then identify and total the current liabilities. Calculate Acme's working capital by subtracting the current liabilities from the current assets.

As a business grows, it needs more working capital. As sales expand, customers owe the business more money. Accounts receivable grow. Inventory usually must grow too to accommodate a growth in sales. The growth of accounts receivable and inventory expands current assets. Where does the money come from for this?

The company is likely to owe its suppliers more as it buys more inventory. So the suppliers help finance some of the growth of assets. The company may accrue larger payrolls and other expenses. Current liabilities grow. Often short-term loans are taken out to help meet the need for expanded working capital.

Current liabilities can almost never grow as fast as current assets grow when a company is expanding sales. So the growth in working capital needed to support sales growth must be financed from some other source. Remember that the balance sheet must balance. If current assets go up faster than current liabilities, long-term liabilities or capital must increase.

Profits are the major source to finance increases in current assets. The company takes its after-tax profits and plows them back into the business rather than paying out the profits as dividends.

Other sources of financing for working capital increases are long-term loans or the sale of additional stock.

Sometimes none of these sources are available. Money may be tight, and banks or other lenders reluctant to lend. The stock market may be depressed, and no stock can be sold. Profits may be inadequate to finance working capital needs. When these situations occur, a company can literally expand into bankruptcy.

This is an important concept. Learn it well. You can go broke when your sales are growing by leaps and bounds. I have acquired several companies that suffered this fate. I have seen many others liquidated or swallowed up.

How can a growing company go broke? Easy.

As sales grow and grow, more and more of the company's funds are tied up in accounts receivable and inventory. Cash to buy new inventory begins to run dry. Suppliers refuse to ship until accounts payable are paid. They refuse to extend further credit. Banks, insurance companies, and other lenders refuse to give the company any more loans. No new money can be raised from stockholders. Profits are insufficient to handle the growth of working capital needs.

The more sales the company makes, the more trouble it gets into. It must buy inventory to fill the new orders and then wait until customers get around to paying. If money is tight all over, customers start slowing down their payments. Eventually, the company actually runs out of cash. It cannot come up with the money to pay suppliers, employees, tax collectors, and so forth.

Sometimes the outcome is delayed by the company's borrowing money at very high interest rates. But the high interest usually eats up the profits that might be used to expand working capital.

A famous promoter once said he would rather be alive at high interest rates than dead at low rates. He borrowed at high interest rates. He went bankrupt anyway.

What can a company do when it is successful in sales and going broke at the same time? Simple. Stop expanding working capital faster than it can be financed.

Collect accounts receivable faster with a tougher collection effort. Cut off credit to slow-paying customers. Demand cash with orders. Shift the sales and advertising efforts to customers who will pay quickly.

Look for ways to move inventory in and out more quickly. Companies are often organized so that there is a long lag from the time they buy inventory until they sell finished goods. Inventory is money. The longer it takes inventory to flow through the business, the longer money is tied up and unavailable. The ideal goal is to sell inventory so fast that you collect from your customers before you have to pay your suppliers. Most companies can't do things this fast. But every company can find ways to speed inventory turnover. "Just-in-time" inventory acquisition is a way to achieve this.

The first way to control working capital is to control the key assets. Accounts receivable must be held in check. Inventory must move rapidly. It often happens that controlling assets slows down sales growth. So be it. Selling more and more to get deeper and deeper into the hole is dumb.

After assets are controlled, you can look to liabilities. If the problem is temporary, perhaps a short-term loan can help. But don't kid yourself. Usually working capital problems are long-term.

Talk to your suppliers. Can you temporarily slow down payments to get a breather? Perhaps a different supplier will give you easier credit terms.

Don't fool with accruals. Delaying payments due to employees or governments is sure trouble. Desperate managers are tempted to use the dollars that are supposed to be withheld for payroll taxes or income taxes. Desperate managers like this often go to jail.

Working capital problems are rarely, if ever, solved by fiddling with liabilities. Holding down on current assets is the primary solution.

Many smaller companies are headed by sales wizards. They really know how to generate sales. But they often get into trouble. Sales wizards usually think that more sales will cure any problem. But working capital problems seldom succumb to more sales. More sales can make the problem worse. And the sales wizard ends up having to sell his company to a larger, richer company that can balance sales with profits and working capital requirements. The sales wizard can't understand what happened to his company. It was going so great.

I hope this is clear. A company that is successful in sales can go broke. Sales must be turned into profits. Sales must be supported by adequate working capital, which normally is built up by profits. If sales grow faster than profits or working capital, a seemingly successful company can go sour.

Average Collection Period

In discussing working capital problems, we touched on the problems of collecting accounts receivable. Now let's look at a useful way to measure trends in collections.

The average collection period is the number of days required, on average, to collect amounts owed to the company by its customers. A company that collects cash when it makes a sale has an advantage over a company that has to wait six months to get paid. A company that took 20 days, on average, to collect its accounts last year and that takes 30 days this year has a problem. If its customers normally owe it $1 million, the extra ten days for collection means that the company is denied the use of $1 million in cash for ten days.

The average collection period is expressed in days. It is computed as follows:

$$\text{Average Collection Period} = \frac{\text{Average Accounts Receivable for period}}{\text{Sales in period}} \times \text{No. of Days}$$

If Acme Widget had average accounts receivable of $80,000 and annual sales of $400,000, the equation would look like this.

$$\text{Average Collection Period} = \frac{80,000}{400,000} \times 365 = 73 \text{ days Average Collection Period}$$

What if the next year Acme Widget had sales of $480,000 and average accounts receivable of $100,000? What would the average collection period be? Is this better or worse than the previous year?

A lengthening of the average collection period can indicate that a company is getting into working capital troubles.

Each industry and company has its own typical average collection period—normally a range within which the average days fall. A grocery store that sells only for cash has zero days average collection period. Businesses that sell large items to governments face much red tape in getting paid. The average collection period for such businesses may extend into many months—even years.

The trend is what is important to a company. An average collection period that is getting longer must be watched. The average collection period can be shortened by collecting accounts more aggressively, by tightening up on credit terms, or by shifting sales efforts away from slower-paying customers.

A trend toward a longer average collection period may indicate a slackening collection effort. Goods may be sold to less creditworthy customers. The trend may also indicate that a fading product line, or a weak sales effort, or tough new competition makes it much more difficult to get sales without giving extended credit as an inducement.

The average collection period is a valuable signal. It is well worth watching in your own business or in one you are considering.

Inventory Turnover

Inventory turnover is another signal that may warn of trouble ahead. We have said that inventory is money sitting in the factory, in the warehouse, or on shop shelves. Inventory sitting idle costs money. It costs the interest on the money used to purchase it. It costs the profits that might be made from selling it and using the money elsewhere.

Idle inventory costs money for storage, rent, heat, power, security, and so forth. Various management consulting groups have determined that inventory sitting around idle costs from 20 to 25 percent of its original value each year. This is the combined cost of interest on money, space, and other storage charges, and the inventory's inevitable deterioration or obsolescence.

Inventory should move in and out quickly. How quickly depends on the industry and the company. A store specializing in fresh produce or baked goods needs to move its inventory in and out in a day. A company making complex heavy machinery may get raw materials or parts many months before the completed machinery is finally shipped to the customer.

Inventory turnover is a measure of how many times (theoretically) a company's inventory is replenished during a year. The formula for calculating inventory turnover is as follows:

$$\text{Inventory Turnover} = \frac{\text{Cost of Sales}}{\text{Average Inventory}}$$

(See the Glossary in Chapter 2 for a definition of *cost of sales*. This topic is discussed in greater detail in later chapters.)

One of the problems in calculating inventory turnover (or average collection period) is getting the average. If you have monthly reports for a year, add the numbers for each month, and divide by 12. If you have quarterly reports, total the numbers and divide by 4.

Often the only thing available is an annual report. Take the number at the beginning of the year (or at the end of the previous year—it's the same thing) and add it to the number at the end of the year. Then divide this sum by 2.

If only one year-end number is available, use that. But be cautious. An average compiled from 12 monthly numbers is more useful than an average compiled from beginning and ending. The latter average cannot take into account possible huge variations during the year. (Of course, average collection period and inventory turnover can be calculated for shorter periods than a year. This may be appropriate for certain kinds of businesses.)

The important thing about inventory turnover, as with average collection period, is the trend. Trends can often be spotted from sparse data. Then further investigation can dig into the trend's meaning.

If Acme Widget had a cost of sales during the year of $146,000, and an average inventory of $29,200, what would its inventory turnover be?

Suppose that during the next year, cost of sales went up to $300,000, and average inventory was $50,000. Would the second-year inventory turnover indicate a better or poorer use of the money invested in inventory?

One more thing needs to be said about inventory turnover. For most companies, a few items produce the majority of sales. (See *80/20 rule* in the Glossary.) This means that the inventory of a few items is probably turning over very rapidly. The inventory of a large number of items may be moving very slowly. Often the slow-moving inventory sits so long it becomes obsolete. If there are enough sales and a fast enough turnover from the hot items, the overall inventory turnover figure may look reasonable. Serious problems of slow-moving or even dead inventory can be obscured.

Inventory turnover is a useful trend indicator. But it cannot tell the whole story. To really analyze a business, you need to get behind inventory turnover to see what is happening to individual items. Nevertheless, the inventory turnover figure can be a help in signaling possible trouble ahead.

This section of the chapter has introduced current and noncurrent balance sheet items. The concept of working capital was presented with the warning that working capital problems can sink companies with rapid sales growth.

We have just finished introducing two signals or trend indicators—average collection period and inventory turnover.

While we have been exploring these side paths, Acme Widget Company has been going forward. The company has now completed its second year of operations. It is time to prepare another balance sheet and then perform some analysis.

5

Still More Balance Sheet

You will be the Acme Widget amateur accountant. You will prepare the balance sheet for the second year. You will follow the same procedures as for the first-year balance sheet.

I will give you the pertinent transactions that occurred during Acme operations in the second year. You will prepare a worksheet that records these transactions, showing each one's effect on the balance sheet, being certain to keep each transaction in balance.

From your worksheet you will prepare a trial balance worksheet. This will put each of the numbers under the appropriate balance sheet heading. Then you can add and subtract to see if the assets balance the liabilities and capital. When you have things in balance, you can prepare a balance sheet.

So get out enough paper for your worksheets and balance sheet. Get out your calculator to do the arithmetic.

Figure 5.1 shows the format for the Acme Widget balance sheet you will prepare. It lists all the items or entries you will be concerned with. You will also notice that this is a comparative balance sheet. The numbers at the end of year one are shown alongside the numbers for the end of year two. This allows you to compare the financial position at these two times.

Figure 5.1 Acme Widget Balance Sheet (Second Year of Operations)

Assets			Liabilities and Capital		
	Year One	Year Two		Year One	Year Two
Current Assets			**Current Liabilities**		
Cash			Accounts Payable		
Marketable Securities			Accruals		
Accounts Receivable			Total Current Liabilities		
Less Reserve for Doubtful Accounts					
Net Accounts Receivable			**Long-Term Liabilities**		
Inventory			Long-Term Debt		
Raw Materials			Total Long-Term Liabilities		
Finished Goods			Total Liabilities		
Total Inventory					
Prepaid Expenses			**Capital**		
Total Current Assets			Common Stock		
			Retained Earnings		
Non-Current Assets			Total Capital		
Fixed Assets					
Less Depreciation					
Net Fixed Assets					
Intangible Assets					
Total Non-Current Assets					
Total Assets			**Total Liabilities and Capital**		

The Worksheet for Transactions

Look at the worksheet prepared at the end of year one. This will refresh your memory on how a worksheet is put together. The transactions at the end of year two often are more complicated. You should break some of the transactions into separate parts to keep them straight. Remember that each entry into the worksheet must balance. A change on one side of the balance sheet must be balanced by a corresponding change on the opposite side or by an offsetting change on the same side.

Sometimes, two or more changes are needed to balance one change. You will get the hang of it as we go along.

Acme Widget Year Two Balance Sheet

1. Acme sells 78,000 widgets in year two, generating sales of $624,000. There are no cash sales, so all the sales are put into Accounts Receivable. The balancing entry goes into Retained Earnings.

2. Customers pay off the $68,000 owed at the end of year one. They pay 80% of the amount they owe for orders in year two. The payments go into Cash, with the balancing entry a reduction in Accounts Payable.

3. Acme begins the year with only 4,500 finished widgets in inventory and raw material inventory for 4,000 more. So many purchases have been made. Acme decides it wants to end year two with enough finished widgets for a month's sales and enough raw materials for another month of sales. (This kind of planning is often important so that the company does not run out of stock.) Sales during the year are 78,000 widgets. A month's supply at the year two sales pace is 6,500 widgets. Acme needs to have available 84,500 finished widgets, less the 4,500 on hand as the year began. That means it must produce 80,000 finished widgets during the year. Acme needs to have the raw materials to produce the 80,000 widgets and have enough raw materials on hand at year-end to produce 6,500 more finished widgets. It has raw materials for 4,000 widgets on hand when the year begins. That means it needs to buy raw materials for 82,500 widgets. At $4.00 per widget, it will spend $330,000 during the year on raw

materials. $330,000 of raw materials will go into Inventory—
Raw Materials. The balancing entry will be Accounts Payable,
because Acme will not pay cash. During the year, Acme will
pay for 90% of the purchases. $297,000 will be withdrawn from
Cash, and Accounts Payable will be reduced by that amount.
The raw materials are converted into 80,000 finished widgets,
reducing the raw materials inventory by $320,000 and increas-
ing the finished goods inventory by $320,000. Sales of 78,000
widgets reduces the finished goods inventory by $312,000. The
balancing entry is in Retained Earnings. (This is a complicated
but common computation.) Remember that Acme must pay off
the accounts payble owed at the end of year one.

4. Acme hires a machine operator at the beginning of year two,
paying the operator $2,800 per month. Each month's paycheck
comes during the first week of the succeeding month. So Acme
will actually pay out 11 months' salary during year two. The final month's salary is accrued and will be paid in the first month
of year three.

5. The owner/managers of Acme continue to receive a total of
$8,000 a month. The first payment is for the 12th month of year
one. Then payments are made in the following ten months for
the preceding month. Finally, the 12th month's salary is accrued
as a liability. It will be paid in the first month of year three.

6. Acme pays rent of $1,000 a month, in advance, on the build-
ing. When Acme starts year two, it has already paid the first
month's rent. That appeared at the end of year one as a Prepaid
Expense. But then the owner offers to sell Acme the building
for $120,000. At the end of the sixth month they conclude the
deal. Acme has paid $5,000 in rent (the first month was already
paid for, and Acme paid for five more months). Acme makes a
down payment of $40,000 and gets a mortgage for the remain-
ing $80,000. The mortgage calls for interest payments at an an-
nual rate of 8%. For the last six months of year two, Acme pays
interest only, $3,200. To come up with the down payment, the
owners each invest $20,000 more, purchasing additional stock
in the company. Six months of rent is $6,000. But $1,000 was
paid in year one. As that month passes, Prepaid Expenses are
reduced by $1,000, and Retained Earnings are also reduced by
$1,000. $5,000 comes out of Cash and reduces Retained Earnings. The six months of interest is $3,200. The interest pay-
ments also come out of Cash and reduce Retained earnings.
The investment of $40,000 to buy stock increases Capital and

Cash. The down payment reduces Cash and increases Fixed Assets. The mortgage increases Long-Term Debt and increases Fixed Assets. The building will be depreciated over 25 years at $4,800 per year. That will be depreciation of $2,400 for the six months that the building is owned in year two. $2,400 is added to Depreciation, a negative amount, because $2,400 also reduces Retained Earnings.

7. Acme purchases used furniture as the year begins for $3,640 in cash. The balancing entry is in fixed assets. This purchase will be depreciated over seven years, $520 a year in depreciation. Only the year's depreciation affects Retained Earnings.

8. Depreciation continues on the widget machine at $4,800 a year.

9. At year-end, Acme evaluates its Accounts Receivable and its Inventory. Management determines that some customers are unlikely to pay. A reserve for doubtful accounts is set up—$6,000. Rats gnaw away at raw materials, causing $800 of loss. Then some finished inventory has become obsolete. $4,000 of inventory is written down to zero. These entries all affect Retained Earnings.

10. Acme continues to have office expenses of $200 a month. This is cash paid out during the month.

11. Acme's advertising expenses during the year are $13,000, paid out in cash.

12. Acme decides to purchase a license to use a new production technique that will improve operations. The license costs $6,000 in cash. It is an intangible asset.

13. At year-end, Acme decides that it has extra cash. It buys a CD for $4,000. Then it pays out a dividend to the owners, $12,000, which reduces Retained Earnings.

14. Then there are taxes. Acme pays the taxes for year one during year two. Its operations in year two create a tax liability of $47,355. This will not be paid until year three. It is an accrual in year two, and it is balanced by a reduction in Retained Earnings.

This completes the transactions that need to be entered into your worksheet for Acme Widget's second year. Go over your entries again. Does each one balance?

When you are satisfied, you can check your worksheet against mine. But I recommend that you wait until you prepare your trial balance worksheet. Find out if you can make it balance. Then check. My worksheets can be found in Appendix A.

Trial Balance Worksheet

Look at the trial balance worksheet prepared at the end of Acme's first year. It provides the format. Of course, you should have some additional headings. Look at Figure 5.1 to see what headings are needed for your trial balance worksheet.

When you have the trial balance worksheet laid out, put in the numbers shown at the end of year one. For example, you don't start year two's Cash with nothing. There was $2,600 in the bank account at the end of year one. Any additions and subtractions to cash in year two will be added to or subtracted from the $2,600 you begin with.

The same is true of other items. Begin with the amount in that item at the end of year one. Then enter the amounts from year two, showing them as plus or minus. Then add and subtract to get a total for each item. Then add them up to see if they balance. If they do, you are ready to prepare the comparative balance sheet.

When you have finished your trial balance worksheet, it will either balance or not. If assets equal liabilities plus capital on the first try, you are doing exceptional work. Perhaps you should be an accountant.

If you are like most people, it won't balance. You should go back over the transaction worksheet and the trial balance worksheet to see what you may have missed. It may be helpful to compute the difference between assets and liabilities plus capital. That difference may be a number that indicates exactly what you left out.

Keep at it until you have the trial balance in balance—or until you are stumped. Then check your work against mine in Appendix A.

The Balance Sheet

Now let's finish the job by preparing the comparative balance sheet or statement of Acme's financial position. If you own this book, you could go back to Figure 5.1 and write in the numbers in the appropriate spaces. If this isn't your book, please don't spoil it for the next reader. It is easier to prepare a balance sheet on a separate piece of paper.

When you have finished, you can check your balance sheet against mine, in Appendix A. When you are satisfied that you have a complete and accurate balance sheet, we will do some analysis. After all, that's what all these numbers are really for—to help you make better judgments. Analysis of the financial reports is the basis for judgments.

We will use the Acme Widget balance sheet for year two to do several kinds of analysis and to make some judgments about the company. So go to it and finish the balance sheet work.

Analyzing the Balance Sheet

You are an owner of Acme Widget. Suppose that a large conglomerate has offered to buy Acme for cash. How much cash would you want to receive to sell Acme?

Your total capital (common stock plus retained earnings) is $217,605. This is the company's net worth, according to the balance sheet. Would you sell the company for this amount? What about adding working capital to that? That is $132,485. But long-term debt should be subtracted. That's $80,000. Capital, retained earnings, and working capital, less long-term debt, add up to $270,090. Is that what the company is worth? If not, how much would you be willing to sell it for?

In considering this question, you will want to think about what hidden assets, if any, Acme has that make it more valuable than the books show. What other factors might influence your decision on Acme's value? For one thing, there is your own personal involvement in the company. That would certainly change if you sold out.

Does Acme have a valuable market niche? An especially efficient process? A loyal customer base? You can think of other considerations that would affect your analysis of Acme's worth. The balance sheet does not tell the whole story.

Let's put the shoe on the other foot. You represent the large conglomerate. Your board of directors has instructed you to make a cash offer to acquire Acme Widget. You have the balance sheet in front of you. Now you must determine what would be a fair offer for the company.

You will want to not only identify hidden assets, but also consider possible hidden liabilities. Perhaps some of the assets are overvalued. It is clear that you will probably end up with a different value when you are a buyer than when you are a seller. Remember that perspective influences valuation. The scores that show on financial reports do not represent an exact and "true" value.

Let's make some calculations. First, working capital (current assets minus current liabilities). What was Acme's working capital at the end of year one? What is it at the end of year two?

The working capital has increased substantially. This is a natural enough result of the large increase in sales—from $292,000 in year one to $624,000 in year two. Has the increase in working capital been proportional to the increase in sales? Calculate the percentage growth in sales and then the percentage growth in working capital. This will show the answer.

Another approach is to calculate what percentage of sales the first year-end working capital was. Then calculate what percentage of second-year sales the second year-end working capital was. You will find that the working capital at the end of the second year was a higher percentage of sales. Is this important? It might be. If working capital as a percentage of sales continues to increase, the company could get into serious working capital problems if sales keep leaping upward.

Now let's compute the average collection period for Acme Widget. Use the beginning and ending accounts receivable for each year to calculate the average accounts receivable.

In which direction is the average collection period going? Is it getting shorter or longer? The company set up a reserve for doubtful accounts. What concerns would you want to express to the management from these signals?

Additional aspects of the balance sheet can be analyzed. Is the inventory worth what is shown? What possible problems might make the inventory less valuable?

The fixed assets have been depreciated. Is the depreciation shown a true indicator of these assets' loss of value? How might the value of these fixed assets differ from what the balance sheet shows?

The owners of Acme put $120,000 in cash into the business. They have retained earnings of $97,605 after the end of two years of operation. How much cash do they have? Is there any relationship between retained earnings and cash?

We will return to the balance sheet later as we tie it into the analysis arising from other kinds of financial reports.

Balance Sheet Summary

It is time to wind up this discussion of the balance sheet with a summary of all we have learned. It is quite a lot.

A balance sheet is a statement of the company's financial position at a specific point in time.

The balance sheet is divided into three sections —assets, liabilities, and capital. Normally, assets are shown on the left side or at the top. Liabilities and capital are shown on the right side or on the lower part of the balance sheet.

The total of the assets must equal or balance the total of the liabilities and capital. If assets increase, either liabilities or capital must increase correspondingly. The balance sheet formula is assets = liabilities + capital.

Current assets are those that are likely to be converted into cash within one year. The assets are listed in the order that reflects their likelihood of conversion into cash.

Principal current assets are as follows:

- **Cash.** Money on hand or in the bank checking account.
- **Marketable securities.** Short-term investments, easily converted into cash, usually used to earn interest on cash not immediately needed.
- **Accounts receivable.** Amounts owed to the company by its customers.
- **Reserve or allowance for doubtful accounts or bad debts.** An amount set aside from accounts receivable to allow for estimated nonpayment by customers.
- **Inventory.** A company's store of raw materials, goods being manufactured, and finished goods ready for sale.

- **Reserve for inventory loss, write-downs, and write-offs.** Amounts by which the inventory value is reduced that represent estimated losses in that value due to deterioration, damage, obsolescence, or other causes.
- **Prepaid expenses or deferred charges.** Amounts paid in advance for goods or services that will come to the company in the future.

Noncurrent assets include the following:

- **Fixed assets.** Buildings, land, improvements to property, machinery, furniture, fixtures, vehicles, and equipment used in the business that have a useful life of more than a year—usually several years.
- **Depreciation.** Depreciation converts an expenditure for a fixed asset into an expense over time. It is a reduction in the value of fixed assets. The actual amount of depreciation is controlled by IRS guidelines and is not necessarily related to the asset's actual loss in value.
- **Intangible assets.** These may appear under various names. Included are items such as research and development expenditures, patents, copyrights, franchises, and licenses. Intangible assets often are not shown on the balance sheet, even though they may be important items of value.
- **Goodwill.** The excess of the cost of assets acquired over their book value.

Assets are put on a company's books and are entered on the balance sheet at their original cost. This may or may not reflect the assets' true value.

Liabilities are amounts the company owes to other companies or individuals.

Liabilities are listed on the balance sheet in the approximate order in which they are likely to come due. Current liabilities come due within one year or less.

Principal current liabilities are as follows:

- **Notes payable.** Amounts owed to banks or other lenders due in a year or less. Short-term borrowings.
- **Current portion of long-term debt.** The portion of the long-term debt that is due to be paid within a year or less—usually included in current liabilities.

- **Accounts payable.** Amounts owed to outside suppliers of goods or services.
- **Accruals.** Payroll, taxes, and other amounts that have been accrued or built up but that are not due to be paid until after the end of the accounting period.

Noncurrent liabilities include long-term debt, bonds, mortgages, and other debts owed to outside lenders and due over a period of several years.

Capital represents the owner's interest in a company. Capital is usually divided into two main categories:

- **Stock.** Common stock and sometimes preferred stock, shares of which have been issued in exchange for an investment.
- **Retained earnings.** The owner's share of the company's success or failure. Retained earnings are what is left over to balance the balance sheet when all other items are set down. Retained earnings represent all the net profits the company made after taxes, less any dividends paid. The owner's interest in a company is also called the equity or net worth. Net worth is total assets minus total liabilities—the capital. Net worth divided by the number of shares of common stock outstanding gives book value per share.

Working capital is current assets minus current liabilities. It represents the amount of day-to-day investment a company needs to finance its ongoing operations.

When the need for working capital expands faster than funds can be obtained from profits, loans, or selling stock, a company can go broke—even though its sales are growing. Companies with rapidly expanding sales can go into bankruptcy. Controlling the growth of current assets, especially accounts receivable and inventory, is necessary to avoid this.

$$\text{Average Collection Period} = \frac{\text{Average Accounts Receivable}}{\text{Sales during Period}} \times \text{Number of Days in Period}$$

This is a trend indicator. It reflects the number of days needed to collect accounts receivable. If the number of days is increasing, a company can get into serious cash trouble.

$$\text{Inventory Turnover} = \frac{\text{Cost of Sales}}{\text{Average Inventory}}$$

This is also a trend indicator. It reflects the velocity with which the inventory investment is being recycled. A slow turnover requires a larger investment than a fast turnover.

Now let's look at some of the other important ideas introduced:

- **Going concern.** Financial reports are based on the assumption that the company will keep on operating in the future with no dramatic shifts or changes. If this assumption is incorrect, the numbers on financial reports are likely to be much less meaningful or relevant.

- **Estimates.** Financial reports are based on many estimates. Some numbers are exact, but a significant portion are estimates. If the estimates are shaky, the financial reports are shaky.

- **No "true" financial reports.** There is no one "true" and accurate financial report for all purposes and perspectives. The same company for the same period can show different profits, different asset values, and different net worth, depending on how the financial reports are prepared. Estimates affect this. Equally important, the purpose for which the financial report is prepared affects the numbers.

- **Hidden assets and liabilities.** Some important things are not shown. Financial reports can never show all the important facts about a company. There are always hidden assets. There are hidden liabilities. Factors such as the quality of the staff, market share, potential new technology, competition, impending government regulations, and so forth are not shown on balance sheets but can have a profound impact on a company's status.

We are now finished with the balance sheet—and much else. You have completed the most difficult part of this book. Congratulations!

What follows builds on the foundation of the balance sheet. With what you now know, other financial reports will be much easier to understand. You have learned the first and most important lessons on how to keep score in business.

And by now you well understand that financial reports are better at reflecting scores than they are at showing real spendable dollars.

6

The Income Statement

The income statement summarizes the results of a company's operations over a period of time. It is also called the profit-and-loss statement, the operating statement, statement of earnings, and other names. It is the financial report that shows the bottom line—net profit after taxes.

The balance sheet shows the company's financial position at one point in time—say, at the close of business on December 31. The income statement summarizes the financial results of operations over a period of time—say, from January 1 through December 31. The income statement can show the result of operations for a day, a week, a month, a quarter, a year, or any period of time.

The income statement is the financial report most often used by managers in business. When financial plans and budgets are prepared, the income statement format is usually the principal one used. In many management positions, the balance sheet is almost never referred to. All the financial information comes from the income statement.

If this is so, you may wonder why we spent so much time introducing the balance sheet. Why did we start with it rather than with the income statement?

As we discuss the income statement, you will see that it flows from the balance sheet. The understanding you developed in your study of the balance sheet will make it far easier to understand what is shown—and what is *not* shown—on the income statement. Like the balance sheet, the income statement is a scorekeeping device. The numbers shown are not necessarily true, nor do they necessarily represent real dollars. Your work with the balance sheet will make it easier for you to understand this.

This chapter dissects the income statement into its component parts. We will start simply and progress toward the more complex. Several Acme Widget income statements will be constructed. Then we will do some analysis.

First, look at some typical corporate income statements. You can go on the Web and access the income statements of any public company you choose. Or look at the income statement from your own company. Get a general impression of them. After you have finished this chapter, you will want to come back to real-life income statements and study and analyze them more carefully.

As you look at income statements, you will notice that they begin with sales. They all end with net profit after taxes, or income. In between the sales and the net profit are all the expenses incurred by the company during the period covered by the income statement.

The Basic Income Statement

Basically, an income statement has four main sections—sales, expenses, taxes, and profits. Sales minus expenses minus taxes equals profits.

Let's illustrate this (and some other important ideas) by preparing an income statement for Acme Widget's first month of operation. The following transactions occurred:

1. Cash was put into the business in exchange for stock. This has no effect on the income statement.
2. $60,000 was borrowed from the bank. This has no effect on the income statement.
3. A widget machine was purchased for $48,000. This has no effect on the income statement.
4. An initial order of raw materials was purchased. The supplier was not paid. This transaction had no effect on the income statement.

We better pause for a moment. All these activities occurred, involving large sums of money. Yet none of them shows up on the income statement. They all affect the balance sheet. This is because expenses are different from expenditures. (See the Glossary in Chapter 2.)

An expenditure usually occurs when money changes hands—when actual cash is paid out. But an expense occurs when an expenditure is recorded so as to affect a company's profits. This often happens at a different time than the expenditure.

Acme made expenditures for the widget machine and the raw materials when these things were paid for. But the expense occurred when the machine was depreciated or the raw materials were converted into finished widgets and sold.

This very important difference between an expenditure and an expense will become clearer as we go along. Let's continue with the Acme transactions in the first month of operations:

5. Space is rented, and $1,000 is paid in advance for the first month's rent. Then, on the last day of the month, another $1,000 is paid for the next month's rent. Only the first $1,000 paid for the month of operations covered by this income statement will appear as an expense on the income statement. (The other $1,000 is "stored" in the balance sheet as a prepaid expense. It will become an expense against income after another month of operations.)

6. Salaries are paid to the owner-managers. The first month's total salary is $8,000. It won't be paid until several days into the second month. Even though it is not paid—no expenditure has been made—it is recorded as an expense of the first month's operation.

7. During the first month, 1,200 widgets are manufactured, and 1,000 are sold for $8.00 each. The customer has not yet paid for them when the month ends. The income statement will show sales of $8,000. It will show an expense for the widgets sold of $4,000 (each widget costs $4.00 in raw materials). The expense recorded on the income statement will not be $4,800 (1,200 widgets manufactured times $4.00 each). The extra $800 worth of widgets we manufactured but did not sell is stored on the balance sheet in inventory. It will be an expense when the widgets are sold. The only expense for this month is the cost of the widgets we actually sold during the month.

These are enough transactions to allow us to construct an income statement.

Sales are $8,000. Expenses are $4,000 for the widgets we sold, $1,000 for rent, and $8,000 for salaries. Total expenses are $13,000. Because they exceed the amount of sales, we have no profit and therefore owe no taxes. Our bottom line shows a loss of $5,000. In the simple income statement format, it would look like Figure 6.1.

Figure 6.1 A Simple Income Statement Format

Sales	$8,000
Expenses	13,000
Taxes	0
Net profit	($5,000)

One thing should be very clear from this exercise. Many important transactions are shown only partially or not at all on the income statement. It sounds simple to say that the income statement shows sales, expenses, taxes, and profits, but the actual construction of an income statement is not so simple.

The income statement shows the sales made to customers during the period covered by the income statement. It shows the expenses incurred during the period—expenses that are associated with those sales or with operations during the period. It does *not* show money received for sales made in previous periods. It does *not* show expenditures made during the period that are not related to sales or operations for the period. It *does* show as expenses items that actually will be paid for later.

The time frame within which the income statement operates is a very important concept. Every income statement—whether for a day, a month, or a year—has a specific beginning and ending. The income statement for that period shows the sales that were made during that period whether or not customers paid for those sales. More important and more difficult to grasp, it shows only those expenses that are associated with the sales made during the period or that are associated with activities going on during the period. When expenditures are made—before or after the specific period—is not reflected on the income statement.

Let's go on. Most income statements have more than the four categories we have discussed. A more common income statement format looks like Figure 6.2.

Figure 6.2 A More Common Income Statement Format

Items on Statement	Arithmetic Involved
Sales	Sales *minus*
Cost of sales	*equals*
Gross profit	Gross profit *minus*
Operating expenses	*equals*
Operating profit	Operating profit *minus*
Income taxes	*equals*
Net profit after taxes	

The sales figure does not necessarily represent cash received by the company. The sales are what have been billed to customers (except in cash sales businesses). In most companies, all or part of the sales are in accounts receivable for some period of time.

The sales shown may not be real in another way. Customers may return their purchases in the next accounting period. These returns will reduce sales in that period. (Some companies set up reserves for returns, but this is uncommon.) To the extent that the sales figure will be reduced by future returns, it is overstated.

Sales may have been made to customers who won't pay. Are these real sales? They are reported like real sales, but perhaps they are something else. Sales figures are not always what they seem.

Expenses are not always what they seem, either. We have already discussed the difference between the timing of expenditures and the recording of expenses. Depreciation is a particularly important example of an expense involving no direct cash outlay. (The cash has already been spent.) Other examples are setting up reserves or allowances, writing down assets, and similar transactions. As you remember from the balance sheet, these transactions decrease assets and correspondingly decrease retained earnings (or profits) even though no money changes hands when this kind of transaction is recorded.

Profits are also not cash. Items such as depreciation and write-downs reduce profits but not current cash. Items that are accrued, such as salaries and taxes, reduce profits, but cash normally is not paid until later. The income statement may show good sales and good profits. But if the customers have not paid for the sales, the profits are not cash.

Acme Widget's First-Year Income Statement

Let's construct an income statement for Acme Widget's first year of operations. The data we need to do this has already been compiled. You will find it in your balance sheet worksheet for year one. (Or use my worksheet in Appendix A.)

First, let's determine what the sales are for this period. Look through the worksheet until you find the transaction that shows this. My worksheet shows this as transaction number 11—sell $292,000 worth of widgets. So the first year's sales are $292,000.

Now we must come up with the cost of sales. This is the cost of the items that were sold during the period. The worksheet shows that we manufactured 41,000 widgets during the year. We purchased enough raw materials for 45,000 widgets. Neither of these items tells us what the cost of sales is.

What is important is that we sold 36,500 widgets. Therefore, the cost of sales will be the cost of the 36,500 widgets that were sold during the first year.

What is the cost of the 36,500 widgets we sold? Well, the raw materials in those widgets cost $4.00 each. At least part of the cost of sales would be the $146,000 of raw materials in the widgets we sold.

What about the cost of the widget machine? The expense for the first year is not the $48,000 we paid for the machine. It is the $4,800 in depreciation. The depreciation expense is the cost of using the machine during this period—that is, the amount of the expenditure on the machine that can be charged as an expense during this period. The depreciation expense of $4,800 might be considered in the cost of sales.

But not the whole amount. The machine was used to manufacture 41,000 widgets, and we sold only 36,500. 36,500 is about 89 percent of 41,000. The cost of sales for this period should include only about 89 percent of the depreciation charge of $4,800. This is about $4,272. What happens to the other $528?

It would be stored in the cost of finished goods in inventory. The cost of the finished goods in inventory would be increased by the $528. When those goods were sold, that cost would become a cost of sales for that period.

To simplify things, we did not do things this way on the balance sheet exercises. We will treat depreciation as an operating expense on this initial income statement exercise.

There is no end to the complications involved with cost of sales. Obviously the widget machine occupied space that was rented. So a portion of the rent should be charged to the cost of manufacturing the widgets. This cost would also go into inventory. The cost would move into cost of sales when the widgets were sold.

Someone had to operate the widget machine. The operator's salary should also be included as a cost of making the widgets. And so on. Accountants have developed various ways of determining when to stop assigning expenses to the cost of sales. These tend to be arbitrary. Find out the system that is used in the company you are concerned with.

There is even a special branch of accounting that focuses closely on the allocation of costs to units of production. It is called cost accounting. We will not cover cost accounting in this book. If you are in a manufacturing business of any size, you will probably get involved in cost accounting. Get one of the many books on this topic, or consult with your own cost accounting people.

For our purposes, we will be especially arbitrary and assign only the cost of the raw materials to the cost of sales of the widgets we sold.

The first-year cost of sales will then be $146,000.

The gross profit can be calculated easily. It is sales minus cost of sales. In Acme's first year, it is $292,000 minus $146,000. This equals a gross profit of $146,000.

Now let's get the operating expenses for the first year. Because we did not put depreciation into the cost of sales, we will treat it as an operating expense during this period.

Go through your worksheet and identify the other transactions that need to be recorded as expenses for this period of operations. I come up with rent, salaries, office expenses, advertising, and depreciation. The total of operating expenses is $125,200 according to my calculations. What do you come up with?

Did all these expenses involve cash outlays during the period? Of the $125,200 in expenses, how much actual cash was spent during the year?

Now let's calculate the operating profit. This is gross profit minus operating expenses. $146,000 minus $125,200 equals an operating profit of $20,800.

Our effective tax rate on this low income was set at 15 percent, and we came up with $3,120 owed in income taxes. Of course, we won't pay these taxes until several months after the end of the year.

The net profit after taxes is the operating profit minus income taxes. $20,800 minus $3,120 equals net profit after taxes of $17,680.

We can check back to see if that figure is correct. Look at the first-year balance sheet. What are the retained earnings? We have said that retained earnings are the net profit after taxes minus any dividends paid. We paid no dividends. So the retained earnings for the first year should be the same as the net profit after taxes for the first year. Are they?

Figure 6.3 puts the Acme Widget first-year income statement into a proper format.

Figure 6.3 Acme Widget Company Income Statement for Year One

Sales	$292,000	100.0% of sales
Cost of Sales	146,000	50.0%
Gross Profit	**146,000**	**50.0%**
Operating Expenses	125,200	42.9%
Operating Profit	**20,800**	**7.1%**
Income Taxes	**3,120**	**1.1%**
Net Profit After Taxes	**$17,680**	**6.1%**

Note: Percentages are rounded off.

More on Cost of Sales

Cost of sales is complicated. Some companies don't even have it on their income statement—not because it's too complicated, but because what they sell has no identifiable unit cost.

Some companies sell personal service—the time and expertise of their staff. These include accounting firms, law firms, consulting companies, research labs, and medical clinics. Such companies have no real cost of sales. The income statement would show sales and operating expenses.

Other kinds of companies also have little or no cost of sales. In an indoor tennis club, the product being sold is time on the courts. The construction cost of the courts is depreciated. There are expenditures for lighting, heat, maintenance, and so on. But these costs normally are not considered costs of sales. Most indoor tennis clubs show a cost of sales for only their food and beverage operations and pro shops. The sale of court time has no cost of sales. Golf clubs, ski areas, campgrounds, and many other kinds of recreational facilities whose main "product" is time at the facility normally do not show any cost of sales for the sale of time.

Many kinds of companies buy finished goods to sell. Wholesale and retail companies normally purchase finished products. It is relatively easy for them to calculate the cost of sales. It is the cost of the finished products that have been sold during the period. (Is the cost of transporting the finished product from the manufacturer to the company a cost of sales? It is often treated as such. But some companies call this transportation cost an operating expense.)

In companies that manufacture their own products to sell, computing the cost of sales is more difficult. The raw materials, the depreciation of the machinery, the salaries of the workers who run the machines and handle the products through production, the cost of the space occupied in production, and so forth are allocated to each unit produced. Then, when the unit is sold, the costs attached to that unit go out of inventory and into cost of sales.

The flow chart shown in Figure 6.4 may help make this process somewhat less murky.

Figure 6.4 The computation of cost of sales

Goods manufactured or purchased	(Affects the balance sheet)
↓	
Into inventory	(Affects the balance sheet)
↓	
Out of inventory to the customer	(Affects the balance sheet)
↓	
Goods sold	(Affects the income statement)
↓	
Sale into accounts receivable	(Affects the balance sheet)
↓	
Accounts receivable collected, cash received	(Affects the balance sheet)

You can see that the income statement is affected at only one point on this flow chart.

In many companies it is impractical to keep track of each individual unit of inventory that is flowing through. Cost of sales is computed from this formula:

> Beginning inventory *plus*
> Purchases *equals*
> Total inventory available *minus*
> Ending inventory *equals*
> Cost of sales

Let's apply this formula to Acme Widget. The beginning inventory was zero. Purchases during the year were $180,000 of raw materials. (Again, we are simplifying by considering only raw materials.) Thus, total inventory available was $180,000. The ending inventory (see the year one balance sheet) was $34,000. Subtract that from the total inventory available. Does the resulting figure give you the cost of sales that is shown on the year one income statement?

This is a very useful formula. Let's put it into algebraic form and then see what else we can do with it:

$$B + P - E = C$$

where

> B = beginning inventory
> P = purchases
> E = ending inventory
> C = cost of sales

This formula can then be solved for any unknown. If you know any three of the numbers, you can easily calculate the fourth.

Suppose you want to know how many dollars worth of purchases were made during the period. Your balance sheet shows the beginning inventory and the ending inventory. The income statement shows the cost of sales. You know three of the numbers in the formula. Now you can easily figure out the dollar amount of purchases.

Suppose your boss tells you to not let the ending inventory be any more than the beginning inventory. How much can you spend on purchases? Well, you already know two of the figures. Beginning inventory and ending inventory will be the same. It is obvious from the formula that your purchases must be exactly the same as your cost of sales.

What do you do if you want to reduce your ending inventory? Look at the formula. I find it useful to change it around so that B + P − E = C becomes B + P − C = E. Then I can focus on the quantity that concerns me—in this case, ending inventory. To reduce ending inventory, you must reduce purchases or increase cost of sales or both. The cost of sales can be increased only by increasing sales. To reduce inventory, sell more, purchase less, or do both. The formula will help you see these relationships and plan what must be done to accomplish the desired results.

This formula is a useful tool in planning, budgeting, and analysis.

Nonoperating Income and Expense

Most income statements add another entry. Sometimes it is two entries—nonoperating income and nonoperating expense.

Not all income or expense comes as a result of the company's regular operations. Such nonoperating income or expense is entered below the operating profit and prior to income taxes on the income statement.

What are some examples of these nonoperating items? If a company has excess space, it may rent out some of it. If the company is not in the regular business of renting space, the rental income would be nonoperating income.

Anytime a company pays interest on borrowed money, this is a nonoperating expense. If a company earns interest by investing cash it doesn't need for working capital in marketable securities, the interest earned is nonoperating income.

Significant entries in either the nonoperating income or expense area need to be investigated and analyzed. They may indicate problems.

Sometimes income statements show an entry below the operating profit labeled Extraordinary Item or something similar. Dive for the footnotes as soon as you see such an entry. The footnotes should explain what it is.

An extraordinary gain often results from a company selling off assets—disposing of a division or selling land or buildings or other fixed assets. If the extraordinary item is a loss, it is often the result of closing down a losing operation and recognizing all the bad receivables, bad inventory, and other overvalued assets that must be written down or written off. When companies plan to lay off workers, they will have severance pay and other obligations. These payments will likely occur in the future, but they are put on the books at the time of the decision.

Acme Widget's Second-Year Income Statement

Now it is time to construct the income statement for the second year of Acme's operations. This will be a comparative income statement. We will compare year one with year two. We will also calculate the percentages of sales for the various items to assist in analysis. Use the format shown in Figure 6.5.

Figure 6.5 Acme Widget Company Comparative Income Statement for Year Two

Item	Year Two	Percentage of Sales	Year One	Percentage of Sales
Sales				
Cost of sales				
Gross profit				
Salaries				
Advertising				
Machinery depreciation				
Furniture and fixtures				
Building occupancy costs				
Other				
Total operating expenses				
Operating profit				
Nonoperating income and expense				
Income taxes				
Net profit after taxes				

Go back to the balance sheet worksheet for year two. Use your own or the one in Appendix A. This worksheet shows all the transactions that affect the income statement.

It also shows a number of transactions that affect only the balance sheet. As the first step in preparing the income statement, prepare an income statement worksheet.

Your income statement worksheet should contain each of the headings that will appear on the income statement. Now go through the balance sheet worksheet. Look at each entry. Decide whether it affects the income statement or only the balance sheet.

If the entry affects the income statement, put the entry that you will make under the appropriate heading on your worksheet. When you have finished, you can add up the entries under each heading. Then transfer the totals to the income statement.

For the second year, we will continue using the cost of the widget raw materials in cost of sales. We will not consider the machine operator's salary, the rental of the space occupied by the widget machine, machine depreciation, and other costs as part of the cost of sales. We will treat these expenditures as operating expenses. (Be careful. In the second year, the cost of sales must include some entries other than just the cost of the raw materials used in making the widgets that are sold.)

To calculate the Acme Widget cost of sales, use the formula B + P − E = C.

When you use this formula, it should be clear what other entries will go into cost of sales in addition to the cost of the raw materials needed to manufacture the widgets sold.

Go to it.

The net profit after taxes of Acme Widget's second year of operations is $91,925. If that is not the answer you got, go back over your figures, because you have made a mistake. Dig until you find it.

When you feel confident that you have everything just right, you can check your income statement against mine. See Appendix A.

Reconciliation of Retained Earnings

Beneath many income statements is a section titled Reconciliation of Retained Earnings. The purpose of this section is to tie together the income statement and the balance sheet. Sometimes the information is shown in a separate Statement of Retained Earnings. Figure 6.6 shows Acme Widget's reconciliation of retained earnings for years one and two.

This statement is self-explanatory. The net profit after taxes for the current period is added to the retained earnings at the end of the previous period. Any dividends paid during the current period are subtracted. What remains are the retained earnings at the end of the year. The number on this statement must be the same as the number shown on the balance sheet, or there is a big problem somewhere.

Figure 6.6 Reconciliation of Retained Earnings

Item	Year Two	Year One
Retained earnings at beginning of year	$17,680	0
add net profit after taxes	91,925	17,680
subtract dividends paid	12,000	0
Retained earnings at end of year	97,605	17,680

Analyzing Income Statements

There are several ways to analyze the component parts of an income statement:

- **Comparison with the previous period—dollar comparison.** This analysis method looks at the dollars and compares. Look at the comparative income statement for Acme Widget. (Use your own or the one in Appendix A.) You can see that sales increased by $332,000, operating expenses increased by $39,520, net profit after taxes increased by $74,245, and so on.

- **Comparison with the previous period—percent comparison.** The Acme Widget comparative income statement shows what percentage of sales each item is. For example, gross profit in year one was 50.0% of sales. In year two it declined to 49.2% of sales. Why?

- **Percentage change from the previous period.** Acme Widget sales went up by 113.7% from year one to year two. At the same time, salaries went up by 35.0%.

No one method is necessarily best in all circumstances. You will want to try different methods of analysis to find out what is most meaningful to you in the particular circumstances.

In general, I find that looking at the dollar increase or percentage increase (or decrease) is most useful for sales. Then the other items can be looked at as a percentage of sales. As sales increase, it is desirable that many items represent a smaller percentage of sales. This is because many costs are relatively fixed. As sales increase, the costs won't increase, or they will increase at a much slower rate. When cost of sales or operating expense items increase at a faster rate than the increase in sales, something is usually wrong. It is likely that too much is being spent to generate the additional sales. Trouble is on the horizon.

Another factor in analysis is deciding what previous period to compare with. If the income statement is for one month, it can be compared with the previous month. Or it can be compared with the same month in the previous year.

In businesses with a consistent and even pattern of operations, comparison with the previous period may be satisfactory. For seasonal businesses, make comparisons with the same period in the previous year. It would not make sense to compare the December sales of Christmas trees with the November sales. It is meaningful to compare this December with last December, assuming conditions are similar.

Comparisons can be made against averages of several previous periods—say, against the average for the past five years. Other standards can be chosen against which to make comparisons for purposes of analysis.

I strongly believe in comparing actual results with planned results. How well did you do compared with what you planned to do?

Actual versus budget is probably the most useful comparison. It is especially helpful in analyzing operations. If things have not turned out as planned, what went wrong? What can be done about it? Perhaps plans need to be changed to take into account changed circumstances. Or perhaps operations must be altered to get in line with the plan. Having a plan is a very important aspect of business success. Comparing actual operations with the plan is a very important method of identifying business problems.

Look at the Acme Widget income statements. Get out your calculator so that you can figure out percentage changes, items as a percentage of sales, and so forth. What good trends or indications do you see? What warning signals do you see? What areas would you especially watch in future income statements?

Complicating Cost of Sales

The Acme Widget operations for year two contain a number of complications in computing cost of sales. We used only the cost of the raw materials in the widgets to compute cost of sales. This is simple. It is also wrong.

The $33,600 we paid a worker to run the widget machine should be considered in cost of sales too. But wait. The widget machine operator made 80,000 widgets, and we sold only 78,000. We can't charge the entire salary to cost of sales.

Let's divide the machine operator's salary by the number of widgets manufactured. $33,600 ÷ 80,000 = $0.42. The salary cost per widget was 42 cents. The cost of sales of 78,000 widgets should contain a cost of 78,000 × $0.42 = $32,760.

The cost of sales would now be $312,000 for the raw materials (at $4.00 of raw materials for each widget) plus $32,760 for a total of $344,760.

The machine operator's salary was $33,600. Cost of sales includes only $32,760. What happens to the other $840?

This salary expenditure is tied to the additional widgets that were manufactured but not sold. These 2,000 widgets went into the inventory. We expect to sell them in future periods. Included in the inventory are the raw materials in these widgets and the salary cost assigned to each one. Thus, $840 in salary is stored in the inventory. It will come to the income statement as a cost of sales in some future period when those widgets come out of inventory and are sold.

In our year two income statement we showed the entire $33,600 salary of the machine operator as an operating expense. Now we have removed the $33,600 from operating expense. This will increase profits.

We put an additional $32,760 into cost of sales. This will reduce profits. But notice that the $840 that is stored in inventory does not appear on the income statement. This makes our profits $840 higher than they would have been under the original way we computed them.

If you want to make investors think well of your company, it may be nice to increase profits by $840.

But you have to pay taxes on the increased profit. So you may not be quite so happy about showing increased profits when you realize that this will result in owing more taxes. In year two, Acme Widget paid 34 percent of its net profit before taxes in income taxes.

An additional income of $840 will result in additional taxes of about $286 being owed.

You have paid the entire $33,600 in salary. These changes in cost of sales on the income statement do not affect what actually happened to the cash that came in or went out. But by resulting in more profit, it means that you will have to pay out more cash as taxes.

You can see that the way we compute the cost of sales has an important impact—not just on the score, but also on real dollars.

There are further complications. The depreciation of $4,800 on the widget machine is surely associated with the manufacture of goods for sale. It too can be divided by the 80,000 widgets manufactured. $4,680 will appear in the cost of sales as the depreciation cost assigned to the 78,000 widgets sold. The remaining $120 will be assigned to widgets in inventory.

Year two profits will increase by $120 as a result. And additional income tax will be owed.

What about the space occupied by the raw materials, the machine, and the finished goods? Shouldn't rent or building depreciation also be assigned to widgets and go into either inventory or cost of sales?

In a large and complex manufacturing operation, a large number of various costs can be assigned to units, go into inventory, and then appear as cost of sales when the units are sold. Accountants and the IRS have general principles and regulations that help guide the assignment of costs.

Many managers want to minimize their tax liability. They want to have as many costs show up as current expenses as possible. They don't want costs stored in inventory when they have already paid for the costs.

Some managers try to store as much cost as possible in inventory so that profits will be larger and more impressive. The desires of these different managers are tempered by what their auditors and the tax authorities will allow. In any case, all insist on consistency. Whatever policies are followed should be followed consistently. It is impossible to analyze income statements or balance sheets if they do not follow consistent methods of handling transactions.

Figure 6.7 helps clarify some of the complications of the flow of cost of sales.

Figure 6.7 Complications affecting the cost of sales

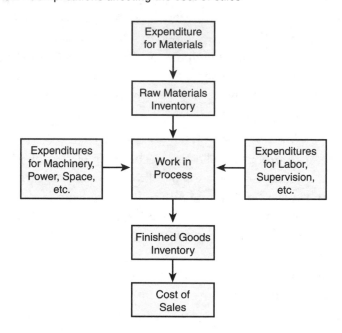

Only the cost of sales appears on the income statement. All the transactions and activities that are shown above cost of sales in the chart affect the balance sheet.

Summary of the Income Statement

It is now time to summarize what has been presented on the income statement. This chapter has been considerably shorter than the chapters on the balance sheet. Yet most managers spend almost all their time looking at income statements—budgeted or actual.

You have seen that many transactions affect the balance sheet but do not appear on the income statement until later—perhaps much later. Exclusive attention to the income statement may not be wise.

The income statement (or profit and loss statement, operating statement, statement of earnings, or something else) summarizes the results of a company's operations over a period of time—usually a month, a quarter, or a year.

A typical income statement is divided into the sections shown in Figure 6.8.

Figure 6.8 A Typical Income Statement

Item	Current Period	Percentage of Sales	Previous Period or Budget	Percentage of Sales
Sales				
Cost of sales				
Gross profit				
Operating expenses				
Operating profit				
Nonoperating income and expense				
Net profit before taxes				
Income taxes				
Net profit after taxes (or income, earnings, or other)				

Few of the numbers on an income statement represent actual cash in or out. Sales are often accounts receivable with the cash collected later (if at all). Some of the goods sold may be returned in future periods.

The cost of sales reflects many expenditures that were made earlier, when goods were purchased or manufactured. Many other purchases will not be paid for until later.

Some operating expenses are prepaid expenses where the cash went out in a previous period. Many operating expenses are represented by accounts payable or accruals. The actual cash will go out later than when the expense is shown on the income statement.

Income taxes are usually payable later. Certainly the net profit after taxes is not spendable cash.

The sales shown on an income statement are recorded during the accounting period, less any returns or sales adjustments during that period.

The cost of sales (or cost of goods sold) includes all costs directly associated with the items that were sold. Which actual costs are included in the cost of sales is a complex matter. Judgment is involved. Consistency is essential.

Expenditures on goods to be sold are first recorded in the inventory on the balance sheet. Then they move out of the inventory into the cost of sales when a sale is made.

Cost of sales for companies with large inventories of many items can be calculated by this formula:

$$B + P - E = C$$

where

    B = beginning inventory

    P = purchases

    E = ending inventory

    C = cost of sales

This formula can be used to arrive at purchases or inventory status as well as cost of sales.

Companies that sell personal services or time at their facilities often have no cost of sales on their income statements.

Operating expenses include all the expenses incurred to operate the business during the period. Some of these are noncash expenses, such as depreciation and write-offs. Others are prepaid expenses, such as rent paid in advance. Still other operating expenses will result in future expenditures, such as salaries or purchases to be paid for in the future.

Nonoperating income results from revenues that are not associated with a company's normal operations (such as interest earned on investments of idle cash).

Nonoperating expenses result from expenditures not associated with a company's normal operations (such as interest paid on borrowed money).

Income taxes are due on the net profit before taxes. Net profit and the income taxes due on the profit can be increased or decreased according to how various transactions are handled on the balance sheet and income statement. Taxes are usually paid after the period covered by the income statement.

Net profit after taxes (or whatever it is called) is the bottom line. It is a score—perhaps the most important score in the business game. At least, it is the score that is most often referred to. But it is only a score. It does not represent spendable cash. The actual cash available may be much more or much less than the bottom-line profit figure shows.

Financial reports usually contain a reconciliation or statement of retained earnings. This shows how retained earnings at the beginning of the year have been increased during the year by net profit after taxes and have been decreased by dividends paid. The retained earnings shown for the end of the year are the same as the figure shown in retained earnings on the balance sheet.

Income statements are usually analyzed by comparing figures for the current period with budgeted figures or with figures from a comparable previous period. Comparisons can be made in terms of dollars or percentage changes, or by looking at various items as a percentage of sales.

The income statement is the primary format for budgeting. The income statement, or portions of it, most often is sent to managers of departments, divisions, and other subunits of companies. It is important to understand how an income statement is put together. It is important to understand what it shows and what it doesn't show. If you are still unclear about aspects of the income statement, skim through this chapter again. Practice with income statements available from other sources. Experience and practice will enable you to deal confidently and successfully with income statements.

7

Return on Investment (ROI)

There are many ways to measure a company's success. The contribution a company makes to society or human progress is one measure of success or failure. Another measure is the satisfaction and happiness of a company's customers or employees.

But in business the score is kept in dollars. We are concerned here with financial measures of success or failure. A company that serves society, satisfies its customers, and makes its employees happy—and loses money—will soon be out of business. The best kind of company is one that can do good in the world at the same time it makes money.

The simplest measure of financial success is the bottom line—net profit after taxes. A company with large net profits after taxes is successful. A company with a loss is a failure. This is straightforward but too simple.

Long ago, managers and investors began to question this simple bottom-line approach. They asked, "What if Company A has an investment of $1 million and Company B has an investment of $2 million, and both companies produce the same net profit after taxes? Are they equally successful?"

The answer was no. Company B needed twice as much investment to produce the same profit or return as Company A. Therefore, it was much less successful than Company A.

The concept of return on investment (ROI) was developed. Companies and their managers came to be measured by how much profit they could generate in relation to the investment they had to work with.

Another important consideration made return on investment a valuable measure.

If an investor could put his funds in safe U. S. government bonds, he would have a return on these funds and almost no risk of loss. If the investor were to put these funds into a business with risk, naturally he would expect a higher return. The higher the risk of loss, the higher the return the investor would expect. Return on investment thus became a method of comparing alternative uses of money.

The investors in Acme Widget put $120,000 into the company. At current interest rates, they could earn about $3,600 a year from very safe government bonds. They could get a return of perhaps $6,000 a year from the bonds of large, well-established companies. Presumably, the investors in Acme expect to do better than this. A new company, especially in the widget industry, can be a risky venture. The possibility that everything will be lost is significant. Because of the risk of loss, the possibility of return must be high.

Another factor favors measurement by return on investment. When all the attention is focused on the income statement's bottom line, a company can get into serious trouble. Remember, profits aren't cash. But it can take a lot of cash to buy inventory and fixed assets. If customers pay slowly, a lot of cash can be tied up in accounts receivable. Assets can soak up all available cash—and more—while a company's net profit after taxes looks great. Then one day the company can't pay its bills, and it goes bankrupt or is taken over by someone else.

So managers must control the investment at the same time they work to produce profits. Return on investment measurements help keep everybody looking at both profits and investment.

ROI can be computed in a number of ways. We will discuss five main ones:

- Return on equity (ROE)
- Return on invested capital (ROIC)
- Return on assets used (ROAU)
- Cash-on-cash return
- Discounted cash flow or present value method

The numbers shown in Figure 7.1 repeat the key numbers from the Acme Widget financial reports that will be needed to compute return on investment.

Figure 7.1 Computing ROI

Balance Sheet

	Year Two	Year One
Assets		
Cash and marketable securities	**$57,640**	$2,600
Other current assets	**166,000**	103,000
Noncurrent assets	**165,120**	43,200
Liabilities		
Current liabilities	**91,155**	51,120
Long-term liabilities	**80,000**	0
Capital	**$217,605**	$97,680
Income Statement		
Operating profit	**$142,480**	$20,800
Nonoperating expense	**3,200**	0
Net profit after taxes	**$91,925**	$17,680

Return on Equity (ROE)

Return on equity shows the amount of profits as a percentage of the owner's investment, net worth, or equity. Return in the ROE formula is net profit after taxes. Equity is net worth or total capital. The formula is as follows:

$$\text{ROE} = \frac{\text{Net Profit After Taxes}}{\text{Equity}}$$

A complication with this and other return on investment formulas must be resolved. When is the investment measured? Is it the investment at the beginning of the accounting period? The investment at the end of the period? Or the average investment during the period? Each of these choices has somewhat different consequences. In relatively stable situations, it really does not matter which is used, as long as comparisons are made on a consistent basis. The examples in this chapter use the investment at year-end.

Acme Widget Return on Equity:

$$\text{Year One ROE} = \frac{17,680}{97,680} = .1809 = 18.1\%$$

$$\text{Year Two ROE} = \frac{91,925}{217,605} = .4224 = 42.2\%$$

Recent industry figures show that the average ROE runs about 12 to 15 percent. You can see that Acme Widget looks like a very good business. (I apologize for having such a high return. When I began constructing the Acme Widget example some chapters back, I did not plan ahead to the return on investment chapter. I would be much happier if these examples were more in the normal business range. But at least you will see how the return on investment is calculated, even if the results are hardly typical of industry in general.)

Return on equity is a good measure of company performance when most of the investment in the company is in the form of equity or when the analysis is being done for the owners.

Return on Invested Capital (ROIC)

Return on invested capital shows the return on the total investment in a company. Return in the ROIC formula is net profit after taxes plus interest paid on long-term debt. Investment is the equity plus any long-term debt or liabilities. Because the interest paid on long-term debt is a return on that investment, it must be added back to net profit after taxes to get the total return on invested capital, which includes both equity and long-term debt. The formula is as follows:

$$\text{ROIC} = \frac{\text{Net Profit After Taxes} + \text{Interest on Long-Term Debt}}{\text{Capital} + \text{Long-Term Debt}}$$

The Acme Widget return on invested capital works out like this:

$$\text{Year One ROIC} = \frac{17,680}{97,680} = .1809 = 18.1\%$$

(Because Acme Widget had no long-term debt in year one, the ROIC is exactly the same as the ROE.)

$$\text{Year Two ROIC} = \frac{91,925 + 3,200}{217,605 + 80,000} = \frac{95,125}{297,605} = .3196 = 32.0\%$$

This measure gives a lower return on investment for year two than does the return on equity measure. With average industry return on invested capital running at about 9 percent, it again appears that Acme Widget is doing a fantastic job. (And the author, less than fantastic.)

In this measure of ROIC, the problem of timing the investment is more serious. Acme's year two beginning invested capital was $97,680. At midyear the owners invested an additional $40,000 in capital, and additional long-term debt of $80,000 was taken on. Retained earnings increased during the year. This made the ending invested capital $297,605. Average invested capital would be $197,643.

The ROIC for Acme Widget would depend on the time period chosen for invested capital measurement. And because the interest ran for only the second half of the year, that complicates ROIC.

Return on invested capital generally is a more satisfactory method of analysis than return on equity. Most companies have some long-term liabilities. For many companies, this debt represents a major portion of the investment. ROIC gives a much more meaningful indication of how well the management is using its total resources to produce profit.

Return on Assets Used (ROAU)

Return on assets used is most useful for measuring the performance of divisions of companies where the divisions have little or no control over liabilities or capital.

In most multidivision companies the corporate headquarters raises the funds and allocates them to the division. Corporate headquarters often decides when to pay off liabilities. The division cannot control all of its investment.

Because corporate headquarters is responsible for borrowing funds and paying the interest, and because income taxes usually are paid on the total corporate results rather than on a single division, the division cannot really control its net profit after taxes.

In the ROAU formula, return is operating profit. Investment includes all those assets used to generate a profit. In many corporations the corporate treasurer controls cash and marketable securities. So these usually are not included among the assets the division uses. The selection of what items to include in an ROAU formula is arbitrary. The basic principle is to include all profits directly attributable to the division and all assets that the division uses to produce its profits.

The general formula is as follows:

$$\text{ROAU} = \frac{\text{Operating Profit}}{\text{Assets Used}}$$

Let's apply this formula to the Acme Widget Company. I don't include cash or the noncurrent assets in my calculations. (But perhaps the widget machine, a fixed asset, noncurrent, should be included in assets used. How would that affect the ROAU?)

$$\text{Year One ROAU} = \frac{20,800}{103,000} = .2019 = 20.2\%$$

$$\text{Year Two ROAU} = \frac{142,480}{170,000} = .8381 = 83.8\%$$

As you can see, the return on investment is quite different with different formulas. ROE gives a different figure than ROIC, which is different from ROAU. Any of the formulas can be useful. You need to decide which is best for you in the particular circumstances. Then you must apply the formula consistently. Do it the same way for each year. The trend or changes from year to year will be the important information.

ROE, ROIC, and ROAU are methods usually used to analyze past performance. The methods discussed next usually are used to analyze future possibilities.

Cash-on-Cash Return

This method of analyzing results typically is used in real estate deals or anywhere else where cash return on cash investment is the important yardstick.

In calculating cash-on-cash return, the return is the cash actually generated by the operation. This may bear little relation to the profit reported.

The investment is the actual cash invested. Cash-on-cash return says, "We put so many dollars of cash into this deal. How many dollars are we getting out?"

We will not calculate the cash-on-cash return for Acme Widget. You can do so if you wish. But you will run into a problem. What is the cash return? Is it the cash actually taken out of the business ($12,000 in dividends during year two)? Or is it the cash that might have been taken out if we wanted to strip all the cash out of the company?

Cash-on-cash return is not suited to analyzing an operation such as Acme Widget or most other ongoing businesses like this. It is much better for real estate operations where money flows out to the owners and generally is not retained in the business as working capital. When money is put into inventory, tied up in accounts receivable, and so forth, it is difficult to figure cash-on-cash return so that it means something.

Still, cash-on-cash return can be a good way to analyze potential investment opportunities. An investor does eventually expect to get cash back for the cash invested.

For example, Acme invested $6,000 to obtain a patent license. How much extra cash will be generated by this investment of $6,000? If the investment will result in a return of $240 a year (a 4.0 percent return on investment), it is probably better to put the money somewhere else.

On the other hand, if the cash return will be $900 a year (a 15 percent return on investment), it might be a good investment.

Cash-on-cash return can be used to compare alternative proposals or to evaluate future projects and opportunities.

Payback Method

The payback method of analysis is not strictly a return on investment measurement. Nevertheless, this is as good a place as any to mention it.

The payback method asks how long it will take to get the money back that is invested in a project. The answer is usually given in years. If a project will pay back its investment in five years, it has a five-year payback. A five-year payback is better than a ten-year payback, all other things being equal.

Discounted Cash Flow or Present Value Method

Comparing projects or evaluating future projects by the methods we have been discussing has two important problems:

- Few projects, deals, or businesses have the same profit or return each year. Often money is lost in the early years. Then the breakeven point is reached. After a period of time, profits begin to come in. These profits often fluctuate. This uneven return makes it hard to calculate a return on investment over a period of time. How are loss years balanced against profit years?

- A dollar in hand today is worth more than a dollar available in the future. Inflation may reduce the value of the future dollar. A dollar available today can be invested in a savings account, government securities, or elsewhere and earn a return each year. A dollar available five years in the future cannot earn any return for five years. How do you balance the value of present dollars against the value of future dollars?

The discounted cash flow or present value method of analysis was devised to deal with uneven flows of funds in and out and with the fact that dollars available in the future are worth less than dollars available now.

Figure 7.2 shows what one dollar, invested at 5 percent interest, will be worth in five years.

Figure 7.2 The Worth of $1.00 in Five Years

Beginning of year 1	$1.00
End of year 1	Interest earned on $1.00 = $0.05
Total amount in hand	$1.05
End of year 2	Interest earned on $1.05 = $0.0525
Total amount in hand	$1.1025
End of year 3	Interest earned on $1.1025 = $0.0551
Total amount in hand	$1.1576
End of year 4	Interest earned on $1.1576 = $0.0579
Total amount in hand	$1.2155
End of year 5	Interest earned on $1.2155 = $0.0608
Total amount in hand	$1.2763

At the end of five years, $1.00 will have grown to $1.28 (rounded up) at 5 percent interest compounded annually.

Therefore, a dollar in hand today can earn 28 cents over five years. A dollar five years from now is just a dollar. So a dollar today is worth 28 cents more than a dollar available in five years, if we use the 5 percent rate of interest. At 10 percent compounded annually, a dollar today is worth 61 cents more than a dollar available in five years. At a 14 percent rate of interest, a dollar can be doubled in five years.

In using the discounted cash flow or present value method, the question is usually turned around. It asks, "What will a dollar received in the future be worth today?"

Look at Figure 7.3. This is a section of a table found in many accounting and business mathematics books. It is also reproduced in greater detail in Appendix B. It is called a present value table. It shows the present value of a dollar received at some future time.

Analysis by the present value method requires the use of a present value table (or a calculator that can compute present value).

Take a look at the present value tables in Appendix B. You will see that they show many interest rate percentages and many years.

In the table, find the column labeled "10%." Go down to the row for five years in the future. There you can see that at 10 percent interest, a dollar received five years in the future has a value of $0.6209 today. To put it another way, $0.6209 invested today at 10 percent interest compounded annually will grow to $1.00 after five years.

Figure 7.3 The Present Value of $1.00

Years in the Future	5%	7%	10%	12%
1	.9524	.9346	.9091	.8929
2	.9070	.8734	.8264	.7972
3	.8638	.8163	.7513	.7118
4	.8227	.7629	.6830	.6355
5	.7835	.7130	.6209	.5674
10	.6139	.5083	.3855	.3220
20	.3769	.2584	.1486	.1037

We said a moment ago that a dollar in hand today would be $1.61 in five years at 10 percent. Let's check this out. Multiply $1.61 by the present value at the five-year 10 percent intersection.

$1.61 × .6209 = $1.00 (rounded up)

Let's do some exercises with this table. If you are to get $1,000 in four years, what amount of money today would be its equivalent if you invested in a 5 percent bond?

formula: $1,000 × .8227 = ?

Your business is making a cash-on-cash return of 12 percent. You can invest $8,000 in a special deal that will pay off in just two years. How much will the deal need to pay off to equal your usual 12 percent return?

Is this a good deal if you get back $9,600 after two years? After all, $9,600 is a gain of $1,600 on your investment of $8,000—a return on investment of 20 percent. Isn't this 20 percent return much better than the 12 percent you want? Not over two years. Figure 7.4 demonstrates.

The total two-year gain is $2,035.20. This is a return of better than 25 percent. You can see that it is better to get 12 percent a year compounded than the return of 20 percent after two years.

Figure 7.4 12 Percent Return on $8,000

Beginning of year 1	$8,000
End of year 1	Return of 12% on $8,000 = $960
Total amount in hand at end of year 1	$8,960
End of year 2	Return of 12% on $8,960 = $1,075.20
Total amount in hand at end of year 2	$10,035.20

You will get more practice in using the present value table in the following examples. The discounted cash flow or present value method uses the present value table to evaluate plans for the future. Here is one case.

Don Baker, owner of Midwest Widgets, comes to us. He would like to sell his small company and retire. He asks if we are interested. We ask for some information. Then we make a projection.

Baker wants $324,000 for his company. He says he will take $96,000 down and the remainder over the next three years—three annual installments paid at year-end, with interest of 7 percent on the unpaid balance. We would have to pay Baker the amounts shown in Figure 7.5.

Figure 7.5 Annual Payments to Buy Midwest Widgets

Immediately	$96,000
End of first year	$76,000 plus interest of $15,960
End of second year	$76,000 plus interest of $10,640
End of third year	$76,000 plus interest of $5,320
Principal of	**$324,000 plus interest of $31,920**
Total payment over three years	**$355,920**

Midwest Widgets has been making money. Last year's net profit after taxes was $44,000. The business has been stable over the past several years.

When Baker retires, his salary of $84,000 a year will end. But we will need to hire an assistant to handle the extra business that the merger of Midwest into Acme will bring. We expect to pay the assistant $40,000 a year. So we save $44,000 a year in salary costs, before taxes.

With our better production control and selling effort, we expect to increase sales with little increase in expenses. So the acquisition of Midwest will add to the Acme profits. Our best guess is that the additional net profit after taxes will be as shown in Figure 7.6.

Figure 7.6 Additional Net Profit After Taxes

First year	$48,000
Second year	$77,000
Third year	$84,000
Fourth year	$92,000
Fifth year	$99,000
Five-year total	**$400,000**

Over five years we will have paid $355,920 to acquire Midwest Widgets, and we will have made a return of $400,000. The return will be $44,080 more than the investment. The return on investment will be 12.4 percent. Is it a good deal or not?

Let's see.

We will make a table that brings all the investment and all the return down to present value. This takes care of the fact that the investment and return are made over a period of time and at varying amounts. By reducing everything to its present value, we eliminate the effect of timing differences.

We must make a decision. At what percentage shall we calculate present value? This is a critical question. If you compare this deal with investing in a bond at 5 percent interest, present value should be computed at 5 percent.

As you know, Acme Widget has been making a very high return on investment. But we have decided to see if the Midwest Widgets deal is a good deal at a 10 percent rate. If it isn't any good at 10 percent, it won't be any good at a higher rate. If it's OK at 10 percent, perhaps we will want to compute the present values at, say, the 15 percent rate. At some rate it will cease being a good deal. Let's set up the table based on 10 percent. We construct Figure 7.7 to analyze this deal using the present value method.

The table has two sides—investment and return. (Or it might be cash put in/cash taken out, or something similar.) The years are shown at the left. We start with zero because the $96,000 down payment is made at the very beginning. "1" means the end of year one, and so forth.

Under Investment we show the actual amount paid for each period. Under Return we show the actual amount received for each period. These actual amounts are multiplied by the present value factor. (Taken from the present value table, years one through five at 10 percent.) The result of this multiplication is the present value of each amount invested or returned.

Ignoring present value, you can see that the return is greater than the investment. So is it a good deal?

When we add up the present values, we see that the total present value of the investment exceeds the total present value of the return—over a five-year period at 10 percent. This indicates that the deal proposed by Don Baker is not a good one.

For this to be a good deal—at a 10 percent rate over five years—we need to reduce the amount we pay to Baker or increase the net profit after taxes we make. It is a reasonably simple matter to try different numbers to determine what would be a good deal.

This calculation is based on three critical assumptions:

- The amount of return or net profit after taxes we can get each year. Our estimate or projection could be way off. We might sell a lot more or find more savings. But any assumption about future profits must be reasonable and conservative.
- The length of time we are willing to consider for this deal. Five years is a very short time for a dam or nuclear power plant. It is a long time for a fashion or fad business. The number of years over which the present value is calculated must be reasonable and conservative.
- The rate we will use to compute present value. If we had idle funds that could earn no better than 5 percent, perhaps a 10 percent rate is too high. If we can earn 20 percent investing the money somewhere else, a 10 percent rate is too low. The rate chosen must be reasonable. Different rates can be tried.

Figure 7.7 Using the Present Value Method

Investment

End of Year	Amount		Present Value Factor		Present Value
0	$96,000	×	1.0000	=	$96,000
1	91,960	×	.9091	=	83,601
2	86,640	×	.8264	=	71,599
3	79,320	×	.7513	=	59,593
4	—		—		—
5	—		—		—
Total	$355,920				$310,793

Return

End of Year	Amount		Present Value Factor		Present Value
0	—		—		—
1	$48,000	×	.9091	=	$43,637
2	77,000	×	.8264	=	63,633
3	84,000	×	.7513	=	63,109
4	92,000	×	.6830	=	62,836
5	99,000	×	.6209	=	61,469
Total	$400,000				$294,684

These assumptions about future profits, time, and rate must be made carefully. In our Don Baker Acme Widget example, we could make this seem like a good deal or a bad deal by changing the assumptions:

- If we assume fewer profits, the deal is lousy. If we assume more profits, the deal could be good.
- If we consider the deal over ten years, it will be good for us. Over three years, it doesn't look so good.
- If we are satisfied to get a 5 percent return, this is a favorable deal. If we need 10 percent or more, this deal won't be to our advantage.

Let's set up another problem. You can make your own assumptions, set up your own table, and calculate the present values to see if it is a good deal.

Acme Widget customers have begun asking for special fluted widgets. This may be just a fad, but the first inquiry came to us almost two years ago. Now a lot of customers are asking for them.

It takes a special machine to make fluted widgets, and it costs $72,000. The machine maker demands payment on delivery.

We will have to hire a widget machine operator to run the new fluted widget machine. The operator will cost $36,000 a year in salary. We have space in which to put the machine without any increase in that cost. We will disregard the costs of power, maintenance, and so on.

Fluted widgets use $4.40 worth of raw materials. The machine can turn out 25,000 fluted widgets a year.

Our regular widgets sell for $8.00 each. Competitors' fluted widgets usually sell for $9.20 to $10.00 each. We plan to sell ours for $9.50 each. Our rough market research indicates that we might sell from 12,000 to 30,000 fluted widgets a year. Somewhere in between these extremes lies the likely sales.

Acme Widget has excess cash. This cash is currently invested in securities that pay interest of 4 percent. But we need to have on hand the cash now invested in securities to buy the machine. Our regular widget business provides a much better return than 4 percent. Eventually, we may want to expand our regular widget business. If so, we will need more money to finance the growth of working capital. The fluted widget business may be an immediate business growth opportunity.

Should we go into the fluted widget business?

First, you must make your assumptions:

- **Profit.** How many widgets can you sell? At what price? When you figure this out, subtract 55 cents for each widget sold to cover variable operating expenses—sales commissions, order fulfillment costs, shipping expense, and so forth.
- **Time.** For how long a period will you do this analysis? Will fluted widgets be a long-term staple product or a short-term

fad? How far into the future do you want to project? Pick a number of years.

- **Rate.** What rate of return should be used? Is the 4 percent interest that Acme is getting from securities the right rate? Or is a higher rate, more consistent with Acme's high return on investment, more suitable? You must choose a rate.

After you have made these assumptions, set up your table. Use a format like the one shown in Figure 7.8.

Figure 7.8 Fluted Widget Deal

Year	Cash Paid Out			Cash Received		
	Amount ×	Present Value Factor =	Present Value	Amount ×	Present Value Factor =	Present Value
0						
1						
2						
3						
Total						

Enter the amounts into the table. For ease of computation, assume that all cash coming in or going out arrives or leaves at the beginning or ending of a year—even though we know that cash will be flowing in and out all year long.

When you have determined the present value of cash paid out and cash received, determine whether you would recommend that Acme buy a fluted widget machine.

My answer can be found in Appendix A. Don't look at it until you have done your own computations. Your answer may be quite different from mine. That may be because your assumptions are quite different from mine. As long as you have used the correct method, your answer is as good as mine. All either of us can say is that, based on our assumptions, this is a good deal or a bad deal for Acme Widget.

This has been a brief presentation on the discounted cash flow or present value method of analysis. Entire books are dedicated to this topic if you are interested. But I have found that the amount of information given in this chapter is sufficient for almost all business needs.

One last word. You can see why this is called the present value method. All amounts are brought to their present values. But why is it also called the discounted cash flow method? You can probably guess. The cash flow—in and out—is discounted or reduced in value if it occurs in the future. The amount by which the cash flow is discounted is determined by the present value table.

Summary

We began this chapter by discussing various methods of measuring return on investment (ROI). Return on investment isn't the only way to measure a company's success or value. But it is a far better method than just looking at net profit.

ROI measures the profit a company generates from the resources it has to work with. ROI is a measure that encourages managers to manage both profits (the income statement) and assets and liabilities (the balance sheet). Problems in either area can be signaled by ROI measures.

We discussed three main ROI measures:

$$\text{Return on Equity (ROE)} = \frac{\text{Net Profit After Taxes}}{\text{Owner's Equity}}$$

$$\text{Return on Invested Capital (ROIC)} = \frac{\text{Net Profit After Taxes} + \text{Interest on Long-Term Debt}}{\text{Capital} + \text{Long-Term Debt}}$$

$$\text{Return on Assets Used (ROAU)} = \frac{\text{Operating Profit}}{\text{Assets Used to Produce Profit}}$$

Return on equity (ROE) is a good measure when the owners are concerned about the return on their own investment. Return on invested capital (ROIC) is a good measure of the return generated by the total investment in a business. It is especially important to use ROIC when a company has heavy debt as part of its long-term investment. Return on assets used (ROAU) is a good measure for divisions where liability management and cash control are in the hands of corporate headquarters.

Any ROI measure is relative. Different industries have different historical ROIs. The trend of ROI is usually more significant than the absolute percentage for a year.

We mentioned cash-on-cash return as a method of evaluating deals where cash going in versus cash coming out is the crucial concern. Cash-on-cash return is especially suited for real estate deals or for deals where profits do not need to be reinvested in working capital growth.

The payback method is used principally to evaluate new projects. It asks, "How long will it take to get back the money we will invest in this project?"

Because a dollar in hand today is worth more than a dollar received in the future, we discussed the discounted cash flow or present value method of analysis. Using this method to evaluate acquisitions, projects, purchases, or operations requires making three assumptions:

- What will the results be? (profit projection)
- Over how long a time do we measure? (time frame)
- What rate of return are we satisfied to have? (interest percent)

With these three assumptions in hand, plus a present value table and a calculator, we can make a sophisticated measurement of whether something is a good opportunity.

Other methods of measurement and analysis exist. You can study this topic further if you care to. The methods we have discussed will serve most purposes. Let me stress this in closing the chapter: Any ROI method of analysis is superior to just looking at profits.

8

Changes in Financial Position

The financial reports of public companies usually contain three main items—balance sheet, income statement, and statement of changes in financial position. The purpose of the statement of changes in financial position is to make clear the flow of funds into, through, and out of the company. In the past, this statement was often called a funds flow statement.

We have seen that the balance sheet and income statement do not show the flow of cash and other financial resources very well. It is not always easy to see where the funds came from. It is not always easy to see what they were used for. The statement of changes in financial position attempts to reveal this information.

Basically, this statement shows the changes from one balance sheet to the next. It is structured like this:

Sources of financial resources *minus*

Uses of financial resources *equals*

Change in financial position

Financial resources are defined as working capital. Working capital is the reservoir of funds circulated to produce operating profits. Funds are not just cash in the bank. Funds in working capital also include accounts receivable, inventory, and other current assets.

Think of working capital as a circulating reservoir. Inventory is acquired. When it is sold, the funds move from inventory to accounts receivable. When the accounts are collected, the funds move into cash. The cash is used to pay the supplier of the inventory. This reduces cash but also reduces accounts payable so that working capital remains the same.

The statement of changes in financial position first tells us if any financial resources have been added to the working capital reservoir—and where they came from. Was more water put into the reservoir (to use a liquid analogy)?

Then the statement tells if any financial resources were taken away from the working capital reservoir—and where they went. Was any water drained off the reservoir?

The statement of changes in financial position then tells us where the financial resources are located in the reservoir. What is the water level in each part of the reservoir?

The typical statement of changes in financial position uses this format or something like it:

Sources of financial resources or working capital:

Net profit after taxes

Depreciation and other items not requiring the use of working capital during the period (sometimes referred to as noncash expenses)

Total from operations

(These two items—net profit and noncash expenses—provide financial resources from the company's internal operations. To this are added other sources of financial resources or working capital.)

Sales of fixed assets or other noncurrent assets

Stock issued

Long-term borrowing

Total sources of financial resources or working capital

Uses or application of financial resources or working capital:

Purchase of fixed assets or other noncurrent assets (The use of financial resources to purchase current assets does not change working capital.)

Payment of dividends

Reduction in long-term debt

Purchase of stock

(If a company buys back its own stock, it is using its financial resources to reduce outstanding capital.)

> *Total uses or application of financial resources or working capital*
>
> *Net change in working capital*

(Recall that sources minus uses equals change.)

> *Changes in working capital:*

(This heading is usually followed by an analysis of the increases and decreases in each item of current assets and current liabilities making up working capital.)

Sources of working capital are profits, sale of noncurrent assets, increases in long-term liabilities, and increases in capital. (Profits may be thought of as a form of increase in capital because they increase retained earnings.)

Uses of working capital are purchases of noncurrent assets, reductions in long-term liabilities, or reductions in capital (through payment of dividends or repurchase of stock).

Let's turn to the balance sheet and income statement for Acme Widget. We will construct a statement of changes in financial position for year two. This will make things more clear.

Use the statement format shown in Figure 8.1. Fill it in from your own reports or from those in Appendix A.

Figure 8.1 Acme Widget Company Statement of Changes in Financial Position

Year Two
Sources of working capital
Net profit after taxes
Depreciation
Total from operations
Stock issued
Long-term borrowing
Total sources of working capital
Uses of working capital
Purchase of fixed assets
Purchase of intangible assets
Dividends paid
Reduction in long-term debt
Purchase of stock
Total uses of working capital
Increase in working capital
Changes in working capital
Cash and marketable securities
Accounts receivable, net after reserve
Inventory, net after write-down
Prepaid expenses
Accounts payable
Accruals
Working capital at beginning of year
Working capital at end of year

The change in working capital should be $78,005. You can check your statement of changes in financial position for Acme Widget against the one in Appendix A. Go back over your figures if your statement does not agree with the version in Appendix A.

What does this statement tell us?

First, it shows that Acme got funds from profits, from issuing stock, and from borrowing. It shows how much came from each source. This can all be deduced from the comparative balance sheet. But it is more clearly revealed here.

The statement shows that a substantial portion of the funds were used to purchase fixed assets—in this case, the building. Dividends were paid. Enough was left over to increase working capital.

The statement shows where the increase in working capital came from. The total increase was $219,645. Some came from profits. Some came from borrowing. Some was financed by an increase in current liabilities. Then the statement shows that $141,640 was used, to purchase fixed assets and pay dividends. The increase in working capital shows that it went up by $78,005.

This statement of changes in financial position will help investors, analysts, and managers see more easily how funds flowed into, through, and out of the company during the year.

Summary

The statement of changes in financial position focuses on working capital as the company's financial resources reservoir. The statement shows sources of working capital—net profit and noncash expenses (especially depreciation) from operations, sales of noncurrent assets, issuing of stock, and long-term borrowing.

The statement of changes in financial position shows the uses of working capital—to purchase noncurrent assets, to pay dividends, to repurchase stock, and to repay long-term debt. Sources minus uses equals change in working capital.

The statement then analyzes the change in each item of current assets and current liabilities to detail how the change in working capital is applied to the specific items.

The statement of changes in financial position is derived from the balance sheet and income statement. Its purpose is to clarify the flow of funds that brought about changes in the balance sheet.

This statement may be used to plan ahead. But it is not as useful as the cash flow budget, which we will discuss next.

9

Cash Flow Budget

One of the most useful management tools is the cash flow budget. Preparing this budget forces the manager to consider many facets of the operation. The cash flow budget draws on information that affects the balance sheet, income statement, and other reports.

A cash flow statement can be prepared as another kind of financial report. It is not found in the financial reports issued by public companies. It would contain more detail than these companies would care to reveal. A cash flow statement also probably would not be of great use to investors and analysts. It is much more valuable as a management tool.

The statement of changes in financial position tells what happened to the company's financial resources. In the Acme Widget statement of changes in financial position for year two, we can see that the company increased its cash and marketable securities (almost cash) by $55,040. This may be enough historical information. It gives the score. But this information format is not helpful in planning ahead.

The cash flow budget is much more useful. Let's see exactly how.

We will look ahead to Acme Widget's third year. We want to see how the purchase of a fluted widget machine (discussed in Chapter 7) will affect our cash situation.

Making up the cash flow budget requires much thought about the operations. Estimates need to be made. Plans have to be formulated. This kind of thinking is what makes preparing the cash flow budget such a valuable exercise.

I will do most of the estimating and projecting for this cash flow budget. But you will still find much to do. Here are the key estimates and projections for Acme Widget's third year:

1. Sales of regular widgets will increase to 82,500 units at $8.00 each, resulting in total sales of $660,000. Widget sales are fairly steady throughout the year. Approximately the same number of widgets will be sold each month. However, July and August are vacation months, and sales drop to 80 percent of the average in these months. Sales in September and October, after the vacation season ends, increase to 120 percent of the monthly average.

2. We will order a fluted widget machine at the beginning of the year. It will be delivered in March. The supplier does not extend credit. We will need to pay $72,000 in cash on delivery.

3. On April 1 we will hire an operator for the fluted widget machine. The operator will be paid $3,000 per month ($36,000 annually). Other salaries will continue as they were in year two. The monthly total for the old employees is $10,800. In December, we hope to be able to pay a Christmas bonus—$10,000 to be divided among the employees.

4. Office expenses of $200 per month continue throughout the year. We must pay $533 a month for interest on the mortgage.

5. We will spend $3,000 for advertising in the months of February, May, September, and November. An extra advertising expense of $4,000 will be spent in April to announce our fluted widgets.

6. Fluted widget sales will develop over time. The first two months we have the machine, no fluted widgets will be sold. The sales by month thereafter are estimated as shown in Figure 9.1.

Figure 9.1 Estimating Sales by Month

Month	Widgets Sold × $9.50 Each =	Dollar Sales
May	1,000	$9,500
June	1,200	11,400
July	1,600	15,200
August	1,500	14,250
September	2,000	19,000
October	2,100	19,950
November	2,100	19,950
December	2,500	23,750
	14,000 units	$133,000

7. We decide to try to hold ending inventory to about the level it is at the beginning of the year. To do this, we will need to buy the raw materials for each widget we sell—$4.00 for each regular widget and $4.40 for each fluted widget. In January, we pay the raw material supplier the amount we owe him at the end of year two. Thereafter we order on a monthly basis. The supplier gives us credit. On average, we pay 30 days after we get our monthly order.

8. The tax bill of $47,355 will be due on March 15. (Estimated tax payments due earlier are ignored for this exercise.) In October we hope to pay our shareholders a dividend of 10 cents a share ($12,000).

9. The primary source of cash will be collections from our customers. Our average collection period has been over 70 days. We expect to reduce that to 60 days by vigorous collection efforts and by selling to certain poor accounts for cash only. At the beginning of year three, customers owe us $124,800, less the reserve of $6,000. These accounts represent sales over the last months of year two. We expect to collect 40 percent of these accounts receivable in January.

Another 40 percent should be collected in February, and the remainder will be collected in March. We will begin collecting for the sales made in year three in March (60 days after the sales made in January).

The cash flow budget is shown in Figure 9.2. I have prepared the budget for the first six months of year three. You should fill in the numbers for the last six months.

You recognize, of course, that this is a greatly simplified budget. We have ignored such important factors as inflation, increased costs due to the installation of the fluted widget machine, FICA and other employee benefits required by law, and much more. An actual cash flow budget can become quite complicated. (Or it can be simplified by lumping together many items whose effect on the totals will be insignificant.)

Figure 9.2 Acme Widget Company Cash Flow Budget for Year Three

	Jan.	Feb.	Mar.	Apr.	May	Jun.
Sales of Regular Widgets	$55,000	55,000	55,000	55,000	55,000	55,000
Sales of Fluted Widgets	—	—	—	—	9,500	11,400
Total Sales	55,000	55,000	55,000	55,000	64,500	66,400
Collections— Previous Year	47,520	47,520	23,760	—	—	—
Collections— Current Year	—	—	55,000	55,000	55,000	55,000
Total Collections	47,520	47,520	78,760	55,000	55,000	55,000
Inventory Payments— Previous Year	33,000	—	—	—	—	—
Inventory Payments— Current Year Regular	—	27,500	27,500	27,500	27,500	27,500
Inventory Payments— Current Year Fluted	—	—	—	—	—	4,400
Total Inventory Payments	33,000	27,500	27,500	27,500	27,500	31,900
Office Expenses and Interest	733	733	733	733	733	733
Advertising	—	3,000	—	4,000	3,000	—
Salaries & Bonus	10,800	10,800	10,800	13,800	13,800	13,800
Tax Payment	—	—	47,355	—	—	—
Fluted Widget Machine Payment	—	—	72,000	—	—	—
Dividend Payment	—	—	—	—	—	—

	Jan.	Feb.	Mar.	Apr.	May	Jun.
TOTAL CASH PAID OUT	44,533	42,033	158,388	93,388	45,033	46,433
TOTAL CASH IN	47,520	47,520	78,760	55,000	55,000	55,000
NET CASH FLOW	2,987	5,487	(79,628)	8,967	9,967	8,567
Cash on Hand—Beginning	57,640	60,627	66,114	(13,514)	(4,547)	5,420
Cash on Hand—Ending	60,627	66,114	(13,514)	(4,547)	5,420	13,987
Additional Cash Needed			13,514			

Let's look at the cash flow budget for the first six months. It is clear that Acme has a cash flow problem in March. The payment for the fluted widget machine and the tax payment drain cash in March and put the company in a negative cash position. Net cash flow in April is not enough to make up the deficit. $13,514 additional cash is needed to pay the bills in March. Now you see the purpose of the cash flow budget. It pinpoints cash flow problems. It allows the manager to plan how to deal with the problems.

Acme has to come up with an additional $13,514 in cash to pay all its bills in March. It certainly needs more cash than this. Some money should be in the bank as a cushion or emergency fund. Acme probably should get $20,000 or so. But how?

More stock can be issued. But a more likely source of cash is a bank. How long will Acme need this money? Can it all be paid back before the end of the year?

A banker would certainly want to know. The cash flow budget for the remainder of the year needs to be prepared to show how a loan will be paid back.

Fill in the remaining six months so that there is a full-year cash flow budget. Then answer these questions:

1. Suppose Acme can borrow $20,000 in March for six months at 8 percent annual interest. Will Acme be able to pay off the loan and the interest? Or will a longer loan need to be made?

2. Should Acme put off the purchase of the fluted widget machine until later? If so, when? Or should Acme borrow on a long-term basis in order to purchase the machine? It is possible that a five-year loan at 8 percent annual interest can be obtained to pay for the machine. Interest charges and repayment of principal would require cash over the period of the loan. Is this the way Acme should go? (Is the present value of the profits that the fluted widget machine will generate greater than the loan's present value?)

3. Can Acme afford to pay dividends? Can it afford to pay the Christmas bonus? Will it need to borrow additional money to make these payments?

You can probably think of other pertinent questions that the Acme managers must face. Working out the answers to these questions will help you appreciate the value of a cash flow budget.

Summary

The cash flow budget is an extremely valuable management tool. It pinpoints the flow of cash into and out of the company. It spotlights potential cash flow problems. It helps determine the best ways of obtaining cash when it will be needed.

The cash flow budget can have various formats. We have used a common one, but not the only possible one. The specific needs of the business and the specific circumstances will determine the format that will best focus on the information needed.

Effective and profitable management is much more likely if attention is paid to a cash flow budget. The balance sheet and the income statement cannot be as helpful in forcing the kind of planning that will avoid the embarrassment of running out of cash. We said earlier that a company can be doing well in sales and profits and still go broke. A cash flow budget can prevent this unfortunate occurrence. For new businesses, it is essential to prepare a cash flow budget.

Figure 9.3 charts the flow of cash into, through, and out of the business. Studying this diagram can help you improve your understanding of cash flow.

Figure 9.3 Cash flow

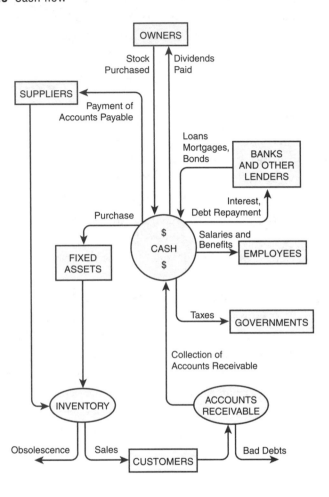

10 —

Other Analysis Ratios and Tools

Previous chapters covered several financial analysis ratios and tools. Among them were working capital, average collection period, inventory turnover, return on equity, return on invested capital, return on assets used, cash-on-cash return, payback, and discounted cash flow method. This next-to-last chapter briefly considers some other ratios or tools used in financial analysis:

- Profit as a percentage of sales
- Breakeven point
- Current ratio
- Acid test or quick ratio
- Debt-equity ratio
- Earnings per share
- Price-earnings ratio

Profit as a Percentage of Sales

Different industries and companies have different historical relationships between profits and sales. Good manufacturing businesses have profits of about 12 to 15 percent of sales. Grocery businesses typically have profits averaging 1 or 2 percent of sales. These figures don't tell us too much. An extra dollar of sales will produce more profit for IBM than it will for Kroger. What we don't know is how much additional investment is required to produce an extra dollar of sales. This is where return on investment analysis helps.

For an individual company it is worthwhile to keep track of the historical trend of profits as a percentage of sales. If the trend is down, look for a problem. A shift in the relationship between profits and sales indicates a need for further analysis. By itself, profit as a percentage of sales is not very important.

Breakeven

Breakeven is a very useful concept and tool. Breakeven is the amount of sales where a company has neither a profit nor a loss. One more unit or dollar of sales, and the company will make a profit. One fewer unit or dollar of sales, and the company will suffer a loss.

Let's compute the Acme Widget breakeven point. First, we will add up all the costs that will not change, no matter how many widgets we sell. These are called fixed costs. (See the Glossary in Chapter 2.) Although no costs are fixed forever, in the short term a number of costs are relatively fixed. In the case of Acme (year two), the fixed costs would include those shown in Figure 10.1.

Figure 10.1 Fixed Costs

Fixed Cost	Amount
Building occupancy costs (rent or depreciation)	$7,400
Depreciation on machinery and furniture	5,320
Interest paid on borrowed money	3,200
Office expenses	2,400
Advertising	13,000
Administrative salaries	96,000
Write-down of obsolete inventory	4,000
Inventory damage	800
Total	**$132,120**

Theoretically, these costs would continue whether or not we sold any widgets. We assume that the advertising outlays, for example, would be spent in anticipation of sales. Salaries paid to the owner-managers would go on. And so forth.

Now we need to consider the costs that will vary with the number of widgets sold. These are called variable costs.

Variable costs will certainly include the cost of sales. We incur a cost of sales only when a sale is made. In our Acme Widget financial reports we have only considered the cost of the raw materials—$4.00 per widget—as a cost of sales.

Is the widget machine operator's salary fixed or variable? We will treat it as variable. If demand were low, we would lay off the operator. If demand picked up, we would hire another operator for a second shift. The machine operator's salary results in a variable cost of 43 cents per widget.

We will consider the reserve for bad debts as a variable cost. If sales go up, we will probably need a larger reserve. If the reserve for bad debts is 1 percent of sales, the cost is 8 cents for each widget sold.

For each widget sold at $8.00, we have variable costs of $4.51. This means that we have $3.49 available from the sale of each widget to pay for fixed costs. How many widgets do we have to sell to exactly cover the fixed costs of $132,120?

$$\$132,120 \div \$3.49 = 37,857 \text{ widgets}$$

In other words, we must sell 37,857 widgets, on which we make $3.49 each, just to cover the fixed costs of $132,120.

How much profit does Acme make when we sell the next widget?

What is the Acme loss if one fewer widget is sold?

Figure 10.2 shows the relationship between sales and profits in a breakeven graph.

The breakeven point on the graph is where the sales line crosses the fixed-cost line. You can estimate from the graph what profits would be generated by selling, say, 60,000 widgets. See the dotted line that traces up from 60,000 units sold, crosses the fixed-cost line, and then goes across to the dollars line. The profit on sales of 60,000 units is $77,280.

The formula for computing the breakeven point can be stated in this way:

breakeven units = fixed cost ÷ (unit selling price − variable cost per unit)

Figure 10.2 Breakeven graph

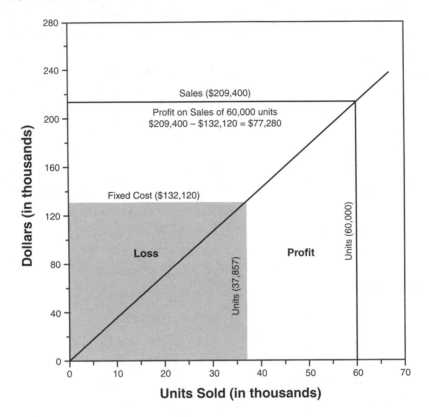

Breakeven analysis often looks at the number of units required to break even and asks whether the company can reasonably expect to sell that many units. If the projection of breakeven point comes up with a number of units that is far too many to expect to sell, there is a problem. Perhaps fixed costs are too high and must be cut. Perhaps the variable costs are out of line. Perhaps a different kind of selling effort is needed to sell more units. Or perhaps the project should be abandoned before it produces a big loss.

Breakeven analysis is one of the most valuable planning tools. Good managers find themselves using it often. New businesses, especially, need to calculate breakeven.

Current Ratio

The current ratio equals current assets divided by current liabilities. Bankers and other lenders look at the current ratio as a measure of a company's ability to pay its debts.

Lenders like to see a current ratio of 2 to 1 or more. In other words, current assets should be twice as large as current liabilities.

The idea of the current ratio is that if current assets were all turned into cash upon liquidation of the business, current liabilities would have to be paid off. Then how much would be left over to pay off long-term liabilities? A 2 to 1 current ratio indicates that current liabilities could be paid off and an equal amount would still be left to pay other debts.

Acid Test or Quick Ratio

The acid test or quick ratio was developed because lenders realized that all the current assets might not actually be worth what is shown on the balance sheet. Accounts receivable might not all be collectible. Inventory might contain many obsolete items. Therefore, a more rigorous measure than the current ratio was devised. The acid test or quick ratio is calculated by this formula:

$$\text{Quick Ratio} = \frac{\text{Cash} + \text{Marketable Securities} + \text{Accounts and Notes Receivable}}{\text{Current Liabilities}}$$

Assets that are most easily converted into cash are divided by current liabilities to give the quick ratio. This ratio must be better than 1 to 1 to pass the acid test.

Debt-Equity Ratio

Lenders and analysts like to see that the owners have a reasonable portion of the total investment in a business.

Some kinds of businesses have long-term debt that is greater than the capital in the business. Real estate ventures usually have small amounts of capital and large mortgages. Utilities usually have a larger portion of their invested capital from debt and a smaller portion from equity. But many other kinds of businesses have a majority of the company investment in the form of capital.

The debt-equity ratio equals debt divided by equity:

$$\text{Debt–Equity Ratio} = \frac{\text{Long-Term Liabilities}}{\text{Capital}}$$

Earnings Per Share

Earnings per share are calculated by this formula:

$$\text{Earnings Per Share} = \frac{\text{Net Profit After Taxes}}{\text{Outstanding Shares of Stock}}$$

This measure is used by stock market analysts and investors. They are particularly interested in growth in earnings per share. This is thought to be an important measure of company performance.

As we have seen, the calculation of net profit after taxes is not exact. Many factors can affect the profits. We have also seen that profits are not cash and are not available for payment to owners of the company's stock. Numbers showing earnings per share must be approached with caution.

Price-Earnings Ratio

The price-earnings ratio (p/e ratio) relates the earnings per share to the price per share of stock. Here's the formula for computing the p/e ratio:

$$\text{p/e ratio} = \frac{\text{Price per share}}{\text{Earnings per share}}$$

The price per share is the market price on the stock market, or the price in an acquisition or some other transaction. Earnings per share can be those for the last accounting period (fiscal or calendar year) or those projected for the next one.

In the go-go days of speculation on the stock market, any stock related to a hot business might have a p/e ratio of 100 or 200 or more. In other words, a stock with earnings per share of $1.00 would sell on the stock market for $100, $200, or more per share.

In the bust that often follows, these same stocks plummet. Their p/e ratios can go down to 3 or 4 or 5. With the same $1.00 earnings per share, the stock could be purchased for $3 or $4 or $5. What is such a stock really worth?

Who knows? A more normal range for well-established companies in more normal times is a p/e ratio of from 6 to 12.

What is a reasonable p/e ratio? It depends. If you are buying control of a company, you are buying the ability to control the disposition of its assets and future earnings. Control is obviously of value. The worth of control can be analyzed by various methods—discounted cash flow, payback, cash-on-cash return, and so forth. A company might be worth nothing or a thousand times its stated earnings. A premium is usually paid to obtain control.

The situation is quite different if you are buying a tiny fraction of the company's stock, as you normally do when you buy a publicly traded stock on the market. Then the p/e ratio depends on what the "market" believes. If all the potential and actual buyers of the stock think the company will grow rapidly and make ever-increasing earnings, a high p/e ratio will result. If people think the company is faltering, the p/e ratio will be low. The p/e ratio is derived from the expectations of the future held by potential and actual buyers in the market.

Experience indicates that a large number of people turn out to be wrong in their expectations. Stocks are seldom worth as much as people think they are in boom times. Likewise, stocks are seldom worth as little as people think they are in recession times.

If you want to gamble in the stock market, other books can help you. The p/e ratio is not much of a tool for financial analysis.

Of the various analysis ratios and tools discussed in this chapter, breakeven point is the most useful to the business manager.

11

A Summary of What You Have Learned

I believe in repetition. Presenting ideas several times in different contexts helps build understanding. (Just as repeating sales messages can help build sales.) So I will repeat the main ideas presented in this book.

Congratulations! You have arrived at the last chapter. Let's review what you have learned.

Accounting is a method of keeping score in business. It uses dollars as the basic score, just as points are the score in football, goals are the score in hockey, and runs are the score in baseball.

The method of keeping score with dollars is what accounting is all about. Certain basic financial reports are used to present the score—the balance sheet, income statement, statement of retained earnings, and statement of changes in financial position. A variety of ratios, percentages, and other tools or equations are used to analyze the scores, just as sports enthusiasts use earned run averages, goals against, point spreads, and so forth.

The scores on financial reports do not represent real spendable dollars available. A major reason for this is that businesses use the accrual method of accounting. Individuals keep track of cash receipts or payments. Businesses keep track of transactions that create assets or liabilities. These transactions accrue to the company or accrue to the company's debtors or owners. The transactions do not necessarily represent the transfer of actual cash money when they occur. Thus, a business's financial reports show transactions or accruals. They usually do not show the actual flow of real, spendable cash money.

Financial reports are not exact. Many of the items are estimated. The estimates reflect the hopes, fears, perspectives, and judgments of human beings. Different people see things differently. Estimates differ. So financial reports for the same company for the same period can differ, depending on who decides on the uncertain items.

Financial reports are made for different purposes. Reports for tax authorities usually seek to minimize the profits on which taxes must be paid. The same reports prepared for would-be investors may seek to maximize profits.

There is no such thing as the one and only, completely accurate financial report. If you know who prepared the financial report, and for what purpose it was prepared, you will have a much better idea of what the real score is.

The Balance Sheet

The balance sheet shows a company's financial position at a specific point in time.

The balance sheet balances. On the left side (or the top) are listed assets (things of value the company owns).

On the right side (or the lower portion) are listed liabilities (debts the company owes). Below liabilities is listed capital (the owners' share).

$$assets = liabilities + capital$$

Every entry into or out of the balance sheet must be balanced by a corresponding entry in another part of the balance sheet.

Here are the principal assets shown on the balance sheet:

- *Cash*
- *Marketable securities*
- *Accounts receivable.* Amounts owed to the company by its customers.
- *Reserves for doubtful accounts* or *allowances for bad debts*. A reduction in accounts receivable to provide for accounts that may not be paid.
- *Inventory.* Goods to be sold to customers, often divided into raw materials, work in process, and finished goods.

- *Reserve for obsolescence.* A reduction in the inventory's value to allow for possible unsalable goods.
- *Prepaid expenses.* Amounts paid for goods or services that will come to the company in the future.
- *Fixed assets.* Machinery, land, buildings, improvements to rented property, and other long-term assets used to create inventory, generate sales, or operate the business.
- *Depreciation.* A reduction in the value of a fixed asset to turn the expenditure made to acquire the fixed asset into an expense over a period of time. Sometimes related to the asset's useful life.
- *Other assets.* Copyrights, patents, franchises, licenses, and other intangible items, as well as goodwill.

The principal liabilities are as follows:

- *Notes payable.* Amounts owed to banks or other lenders, due within a year or less.
- *Accounts payable.* Amounts owed to suppliers of goods or services to the company.
- *Accruals.* Usually salaries and benefits owed to employees but not yet paid. Also taxes owed, although sometimes taxes owed are a separate entry.
- *Long-term liabilities.* Bonds, long-term loans, mortgages not due for more than a year.

Here are the principal items of capital:

- *Capital stock.* Preferred and common shares of stock issued and sold to investors who become owners.
- *Retained earnings.* A company's accumulated after-tax profits less any dividends paid; not available cash.

Assets are listed in the order in which they can be converted into cash. Liabilities are listed in the order in which they are due for payment. Current assets are those likely to become cash within one year. Current liabilities are debts due within one year.

Working capital equals current assets minus current liabilities. Working capital represents the funds available in a business that circulate to produce profits. As the business operates, the funds in working capital flow from inventory to accounts receivable to cash to accounts payable to inventory.

Current assets divided by current liabilities equals the current ratio. Lenders like to see a current ratio of at least 2 to 1. This indicates a company's ability to pay off its loans.

All items are entered onto the balance sheet at their original cost. Adjustments may be made to reduce value, but increases in value are not recognized on financial reports.

Reductions in value come from three principal sources.

Reserves for doubtful accounts or allowances for bad debts are reductions in accounts receivable caused by customers' inability or unwillingness to pay their bills.

Inventory obsolescence or reserves for obsolescence are reductions in the value of inventory. The likely cause of obsolescence is items in the inventory that are going out of style or being shoved aside by more competitive products.

Depreciation or amortization is the reduction in value of fixed assets or other assets over a period of time. The amount of time is related to useful life and IRS regulations. A machine with a useful life of ten years will have its value reduced to zero (or scrap value) over a period of ten years. The purchase of the machine is an expenditure. The machine's depreciation is an expense entered over a ten-year period. Depreciation is a major item that affects the relationship of actual cash to financial scores.

The reserve for doubtful accounts is an estimate. It may be wrong. With companies in trouble, the reserve is often understated. Inventory obsolescence is also an estimate. Companies in trouble seldom recognize the true extent of obsolescence. Depreciation is also an estimate. A machine, building, or other fixed asset may have a much shorter or much longer useful life than anticipated (or allowed for depreciation purposes by the IRS). If the fixed asset is good only for producing unsalable goods, it has no value, no matter how new it is. On the other hand, many companies have assets that keep generating profits long after they have been depreciated to zero. Some assets, such as buildings, may grow in value with inflation or changes in market conditions. An increase in real value can occur at the same time depreciation is reducing book value.

When looking at a balance sheet, determine whether any assets are valued at more than their true worth. Also determine what assets may be valued at less than their true worth.

Then ask what valuable assets are not shown on the balance sheet. Most companies do not show many key assets on the balance sheet— software, special production processes, market position, customer loyalty, and especially the knowledge, experience, and capability of the employees who make the company go.

A company's net worth or book value equals assets minus liabilities (as shown on the balance sheet). But this computation of net worth or book value or owners' equity is not necessarily what the owners would sell the company for. It is also not necessarily what a buyer would pay to acquire the company.

The balance sheet and other financial reports are based on certain assumptions:

- The company is a going concern that will continue in business.
- The estimates used in the report are essentially correct.
- The perspective of the report reader is the same as the perspective of the report preparer.
- All entries are entered at original cost.

If these assumptions are unjustified, the balance sheet can be very misleading.

Let me offer a cautionary note. A company can have so much money tied up in assets that it is unable to pay its bills, even when sales are terrific and profits look good. If customers pay slowly, if too much money is tied up in inventory that doesn't sell quickly, or if the money put into fixed assets is too great, a company can be flat broke when its managers think it is doing well.

The balance sheet is often ignored by people who want to see the "bottom line." I hope I have convinced you of the importance of balance sheet analysis.

The Income Statement

The income statement summarizes the results of a company's operations over a period of time. The "bottom line"—net profit after taxes—appears on the income statement.

The income statement usually follows the format shown in Figure 11.1.

Figure 11.1 Income Statement Format

Item	Arithmetic
Sales	*minus*
Cost of sales	*equals*
Gross profit	*minus*
Operating expenses	*equals*
Operating profit	*plus*
Nonoperating income	*minus*
Nonoperating expenses	*equals*
Net profit before taxes	*minus*
Income taxes	*equals*
Net profit after taxes	

Sales are the delivery of goods or services to customers who agree to pay for them. The customers may or may not actually pay. They often do not pay during the period covered by the income statement.

Cost of sales (cost of goods sold) includes the main identifiable costs of the goods sold to the customers. (When only services or time are sold, usually no cost of sales or gross profit is shown on the income statement.) The costs in cost of sales are associated with goods sold. Goods produced or acquired, but not sold during the period, do not result in a cost of sales. They result in a cost of sales only in the period in which they are sold. Until then they sit in inventory.

Cost of sales, purchases, and inventory are related in a simple equation:

beginning inventory + purchases – ending inventory = cost of sales

This formula is useful in projecting purchase requirements, ending inventory, and cost of sales:

gross profit equals sales minus cost of sales

Operating expenses include the expenses incurred to generate sales, fulfill orders, collect from customers, keep the accounts, and so forth. Many of these expenses are cash expenditures during the period. But some are expenditures that have occurred or will occur in other periods.

Depreciation, amortization, additions to reserves, write-downs, and write-offs of obsolete inventory, bad debts, or worthless assets of other kinds are also expenses. These expenses do not require the expenditure of cash during the period.

Nonoperating income is income that arises from sources that are not part of the business's regular operations. Nonoperating expense is most often interest paid to borrow money.

Income taxes are the taxes owed to various government taxing bodies on the net profit before taxes for the period.

Net profit after taxes is the final result of all the subtractions and additions on the income statement. Net profit after taxes is not spendable cash. Actual cash generated by operations may be much more or much less.

The statement of retained earnings or reconciliation of retained earnings shows how the retained earnings on the balance sheet have changed as a result of activities during the period (see Figure 11.2).

Figure 11.2 Statement of Retained Earnings or Reconciliation of Retained Earnings

Item	Arithmetic
Beginning retained earnings	*plus*
Net profit after taxes	*minus*
Dividends paid	*equals*
Ending retained earnings	

Remember, retained earnings aren't spendable cash either.

The income statement is usually the main format used for budgeting. It is important, but keep in mind that various transactions of importance affect the balance sheet but not the income statement.

Statement of Changes in Financial Position

This statement shows how funds flowed into, through, and out of the company during the period. It focuses on working capital as the reservoir of funds. The statement follows this format:

> Sources of working capital
>> Net profit after taxes +
>> Depreciation and noncash expenses =
> Total from operations +
>> Sale of fixed assets or other noncurrent assets +
>> Stock issued +
>> Long-term borrowing =
> Total sources of working capital
> Uses of working capital
>> Purchase of fixed assets or other noncurrent assets
>> Payments of dividends
>> Reduction of long-term debt
>> Purchase of stock
> Total uses of working capital
> Net change in working capital
>> Analysis of changes in working capital items

The statement of changes in financial position is derived from the balance sheet and income statement. It clarifies the flow of funds that brought about changes in the balance sheet.

Cash Flow Budget

The cash flow statement or budget normally is not shown. It does not appear in public financial reports. But it is an extremely valuable management planning tool. It pinpoints the expected flow of cash into and out of the business. It spotlights likely cash flow problems and allows managers to avoid embarrassment, not to mention bankruptcy. Various formats can be used. A monthly chart showing cash taken in and cash paid out is often the most helpful.

Analyzing Financial Reports

Analyzing comparative reports improves understanding. There are several types of comparisons.

Comparison with the past shows current figures alongside figures from the past. What past? This depends on your needs. It may be the immediately preceding period. If the report is for a period shorter than a year, it may be compared with the similar period in the previous year. Or the comparison may be with an average of past periods.

Comparing actual figures with budgeted or planned figures is especially valuable. For managers, there is no substitute for comparing what actually happened with what you planned or expected to happen. You should carefully study significant variances from the plan or budget to determine what changes are necessary.

Showing each item as a percentage of sales helps in analysis. If operating expenses were 52 percent of sales this year and 60 percent of sales last year, this is much more meaningful than knowing that operating expenses were $1,387,000 this year and $1,386,000 last year.

Dollar changes from one period to the next are often shown. Even more useful are percentage changes. It helps to see that sales went up 12 percent while operating profit increased by 18 percent.

When percentages are not given on financial reports, it helps to compute them before you do an analysis:

$$\text{Average Collection Period} = \frac{\text{Average Accounts Receivable}}{\text{Annual Sales}} \times 365$$

Average collection period is the number of days required, on average, to collect amounts that customers owe the company. Changes in average collection period can signal developing problems that may lead to serious cash shortages. Think of the 80/20 rule. Some customers may pay promptly. Others may pay slowly or not at all. Where the trend indicates a problem, it is useful to dig into specific customer payment patterns:

$$\text{Inventory Turnover} = \frac{\text{Cost of Sales}}{\text{Average Inventory}}$$

Inventory turnover tells how many times (theoretically) a company's inventory is replenished during the year. The faster inventory turns over, the less investment is required to operate the business. Changes in inventory turnover can signal problems with inventory obsolescence or sales efforts. High inventory turnover does not necessarily mean that all items in inventory are selling satisfactorily. Again, think of the 80/20 rule. Concentration of sales may mean that a few items are selling very quickly (turning over rapidly) while many others just lie there.

Return on investment (ROI) is the best overall way to analyze a company's or division's financial performance. ROI indicates how well the business is using its resources to produce profits. There are several principal ways to compute return on investment:

$$\text{1. Return on Equity} = \frac{\text{Net Profit After Taxes}}{\text{Owner's Equity}}$$

Return on equity (ROE) is a good method of analyzing whether the owner's investment is being used effectively to produce profits:

$$\text{2. Return on Invested Capital} = \frac{\text{Net Profit After Taxes + Interest on Long-Term Debt}}{\text{Capital + Long-Term Debt}}$$

Return on invested capital (ROIC) is particularly useful in analyzing companies that have a significant amount of long-term debt. It looks at the total investment rather than only a portion of it.

$$3. \ \text{Return on Assets Used} = \frac{\text{Operating Profit}}{\text{Assets Used to Generate Operating Profit}}$$

Return on assets used (ROAU) is used to analyze divisions or departments of companies where headquarters controls liabilities and capital.

All ROI formulas produce percentages. These percentages can be compared with industry ROI percentages, with the company's historical ROI percentages, with budgeted ROI percentages, or with ROI percentages likely from other uses of investment funds. These comparisons of ROI percentages are much more meaningful than a bare percentage by itself. The trends are often more important than the ROI for a single period.

Other measures are used to analyze potential opportunities:

$$\text{Cash-on-Cash Return} = \frac{\text{Cash Taken Out}}{\text{Cash Put In}}$$

Cash-on-cash return is most often used in real estate or similar operations where little or no cash is kept in the business. Cash-on-cash return gets around the effects of depreciation and other noncash items that affect other ROI formulas.

Payback period is an offshoot of cash analysis. It looks at opportunities and asks, "How long will it take to pay back this investment? How soon can we get our money back?"

A dollar in hand today is worth more than a dollar that becomes available in the future. In business, investments are always being made today to produce returns in the future. The returns from these investments are often uneven. A method has been developed to analyze these investments—the discounted cash flow or present value method.

The discounted cash flow or present value method brings all investments, expenditures, and returns to their current (today) value. It *discounts* future expenditures and earnings to *present* value. A sophisticated electronic calculator or the tables found in Appendix B (and in many other books) are needed to calculate present values.

Present values depend on three assumptions:

- The investments, expenditures, and return that can be expected in the future. Usually these can only be estimated.
- The length of time over which the deal will be analyzed. A deal that looks great over a 40-year span may look awful over a three-year span.
- The rate of interest that will be used to compute present value. This may be the interest rate that can be earned with alternative investments or the rate of return the company expects for its investments.

When these assumptions are made, present values can be calculated, and judgments can be made. The discounted cash flow or present value method is a sophisticated and valuable tool of analysis. But it is only as good as the assumptions that underlie the calculations.

Profit as a percentage of sales is a frequently reported number. It has a rough-and-ready usefulness in indicating trends and performance. But industries and companies vary greatly. Return on investment is a much more significant figure.

Breakeven point is the amount of sales that will just cover fixed and variable costs. More sales will produce a profit. Fewer sales will produce a loss. Breakeven is usually stated in terms of number of units or dollars that must be sold. It is a valuable management planning tool.

Lenders like to look at the current ratio. More-conservative lenders apply the acid test or compute the quick ratio. This is a more rigorous measure of a company's ability to pay its debts.

$$\text{Acid Test Ratio} = \frac{\text{Cash} + \text{Marketable Securities} + \text{Accounts Receivable}}{\text{Current Liabilities}}$$

Earnings per share, book value per share, and the price-earnings ratio are often used to analyze publicly traded stocks. However, these analysis tools are not much help in managing a company. Stockholders, security analysts, and some managers think these numbers are more important than they really are.

Conclusion

In this book I have tried to cover the financial terms, concepts, formulas, equations, reports, comparisons, and ideas that I have found useful in a long life in business.

This is certainly not all there is to know about financial reports and their analysis. But it is enough. It is all that needs to be covered in this book. Libraries and bookstores are packed with much longer books that cover these topics—and many other topics in accounting—in much greater, even exhaustive, detail. Of course, the Web has many information sources. If you have gotten this far, you should have no trouble getting help from these sources when you need it.

If you have gotten this far, you should suffer no embarrassment in talking with accountants. Ask them when you need help. After all, they are professionals. They know more than you do about accounting. But you must know enough to ask the right questions and understand and interpret the answers. You should now know enough to be able to do this.

Whenever you feel shaky, run through the Glossary quickly. Go over the summary section of each chapter. Look in the index for the pages on which you can get a review of a specific item. This kind of quick refresher can shore you up when you need help. This book has been a study tool. Now it should be a reference guide.

Let me close with two final thoughts:

- Remember that financial reports are not exact and the numbers are not real cash. Financial reports are scorecards—made up of estimates, structured in terms of a specific perspective, and designed for purposes that may differ from yours. Financial reports are primarily means of presenting scores in business. Do not be fooled into believing they tell the full truth. Don't take financial reports for more than they really are.

- Remember that financial reports are not the only measure of what is valuable. The worth of human beings is not shown in financial reports. Love and truth and beauty and adventure and justice and many more of life's most important things cannot be pinned down by the numbers on financial reports.

Never let your life be dominated by the numbers on financial reports. Use them as tools to help you achieve important and worthwhile goals. Financial reports are unsuitable tools for many of life's most important goals.

When you are on your deathbed, you won't want to summarize your life by saying you had the best ROI, the soundest balance sheet, or the largest net profit after taxes. Keep your mind on the things you will want to look back on with pride as your life draws to a close. I don't think financial reports or accounting results will be among those things.

Thank you for your attention, and good luck with your future in business.

Acme Widget Company

Acme Widget Year One

Acme Widget Year One Balance Sheet Worksheet

1. $80,000 stock sale:
   + $80,000 cash / + $80,000 common stock

2. Borrow $60,000:
   + $60,000 cash / + $60,000 notes payable

3. Purchase machine:
   + $48,000 fixed assets / + $48,000 accounts payable

4. Purchase raw materials:
   + $20,000 inventory—raw materials / + $20,000 accounts payable

5. Pay rent advance:
   − $1,000 cash / + $1,000 prepaid expenses

6. Repay bank loan:
   − $60,000 cash / − $60,000 notes payable

7. Pay for machine:
   − $48,000 cash / − $48,000 accounts payable

8. Pay for raw materials:
   − $20,000 cash / − $20,000 accounts payable

9. Purchase $160,000 worth of raw materials:
   + $160,000 inventory—raw materials / + $160,000 accounts payable
   Pay for $120,000:
   − $120,000 cash / − $120,000 accounts payable

10. Manufacture 41,000 widgets:
+ $164,000 inventory—finished goods / – $164,000 inventory—raw materials

11. 36,500 widgets sold:
– $146,000 inventory—finished goods / – $146,000 retained earnings
Sell $292,000 worth of widgets:
+ $292,000 accounts receivable / + $292,000 retained earnings
Customers pay $224,000:
+ $224,000 cash / – $224,000 accounts receivable

12. Depreciate machine:
– $4,800 depreciation of fixed assets / – $4,800 retained earnings

13. First month's prepaid rent used:
– $1,000 prepaid expenses / – $1,000 retained earnings

14. Eleven months' rent and one month's advance paid at $1,000 per month:
– $12,000 cash / – $11,000 retained earnings / + $1,000 prepaid expenses

15. Salaries at $4,000 per month, last month owed:
– $88,000 cash / + $8,000 accrual / – $96,000 retained earnings

16. Office expenses of $200 a month:
– $2,400 cash / – $2,400 retained earnings

17. $10,000 advertising:
– $10,000 cash / – $10,000 retained earnings

18. Income taxes of $3,120 due:
+ $3,120 accruals / – $3,120 retained earnings

Acme Widget Year One Trial Balance Worksheet

Assets

Cash	Accounts Receivable	Inventory Raw Materials	Inventory Finished Goods
+ 80,000	+ 292,000	+ 20,000	+ 164,000
+ 60,000	– 224,000	+ 160,000	– 146,000
– 1,000	+ 68,000	– 164,000	+ 18,000
– 60,000		+ 16,000	
– 48,000			
– 20,000			
– 120,000			
+ 224,000			
– 12,000			
– 88,000			
– 2,400			
– 10,000			
+ 2,600			

Prepaid Expenses	Fixed Assets	Depreciation
+ 1,000	+ 48,000	– 4,800
– 1,000		
+ 1,000		
+ 1,000		

TOTAL ASSETS

148,800

Liabilities

Accounts Payable	Notes Payable	Accruals
+ 48,000	+ 60,000	+ 8,000
+ 20,000	– 60,000	+ 3,120
– 48,000	0	+ 11,120
– 20,000		
+ 160,000		
– 120,000		
+ 40,000		

TOTAL LIABILITIES

51,120

Capital

Common Stock	Retained Earnings
+80,000	−146,000
	+ 292,000
	−4,800
	− 11,000
	− 1,000
	− 96,000
	− 2,400
	− 10,000
	− 3,120
	+ 17,680

	TOTAL CAPITAL
	97,680
	TOTAL LIABILITIES AND CAPITAL
	148,800

Acme Widget Company Balance Sheet End of First Year of Operations

Assets			Liabilities and Capital	
			LIABILITIES	
Cash		$2,600	Accounts payable	$40,000
Accounts receivable		68,000	Notes payable	0
Inventory			Accruals	11,120
Raw materials	16,000		**Total liabilities**	$51,120
Finished goods	18,000			
Total		34,000		
Prepaid expenses		1,000		
Fixed assets	48,000		CAPITAL	
Less			Common stock	$80,000
Depreciation	4,800		Retained earnings	17,680
Net fixed assets		43,200	**Total capital**	$97,680
Total assets		$148,800	**Total liabilities and capital**	$148,800

Acme Widget Year Two

Acme Widget Year Two Balance Sheet Worksheet

1. Sell 78,000 widgets:

   +$624,000 accounts receivable / +$624,000 retained earnings

2. Customer payments:

   + $68,000 cash / – $68,000 accounts receivable

   + $499,200 cash / – $499,200 accounts receivable

3. Inventory:

   Buy + $330,000 inventory—raw materials / + $330,000 accounts payable

   Pay – $40,000 cash / – $40,000 prior year accounts payable

   Pay – $297,000 cash / – $297,000 accounts payable

   Transfer – $320,000 inventory—raw materials / + $320,000 inventory—finished goods

   Sell – $312,000 inventory—finished goods / – $312,000 retained earnings

4. Machine operator:

   – $30,800 cash / – $30,800 retained earnings

   + $2,800 accruals / – $2,800 retained earnings

5. Owners:

   – $8,000 cash / – $8,000 accruals

   – $88,000 cash / – $88,000 retained earnings

   + $8,000 accruals / – $8,000 retained earnings

6. Building:

   Rent – $1,000 prepaid expenses/ – $1,000 retained earnings

   Rent – $5,000 cash / – $5,000 retained earnings

   Purchase – $40,000 cash / + $40,000 fixed assets

   + $80,000 long-term debt / + $80,000 fixed assets

   Interest – $3,200 cash / – $3,200 retained earnings

   Depreciation – $2,400 depreciation / – $2,400 retained earnings

7. Furniture:

   Purchase – $3,640 cash / + $3,640 fixed assets

   Depreciation – $520 depreciation / – $520 retained earnings

8. Machine:

   – $4,800 depreciation / – $4,800 retained earnings

9. Reserve:

   – $6,000 accounts receivable / – $6,000 retained earnings
   Write-off – $800 inventory—raw materials / – $800 retained
   earnings
   –$4,000 inventory—finished goods / – $4,000 retained
   earnings

10. Office expenses:
    – $2,400 cash / – $2,400 retained earnings

11. Advertising:
    – $13,000 cash / – $13,000 retained earnings

12. License:
    – $6,000 cash / + $6,000 intangible assets

13. CD:
    – $4,000 cash / + $4,000 marketable security

14. Common stock:
    Investment + $40,000 cash / + $40,000 capital
    Dividends – $12,000 cash / – $12,000 retained earnings

15. Taxes:
    – $3,120 cash / – $3,120 accruals
    + $47,355 accruals / – $47,355 retained earnings

Acme Widget Year Two Trial Balance Worksheet

Assets			

Cash	Marketable Securities	Accounts Receivable	Reserve for Doubtful Accounts
+ 2,600	—	+ 68,000	—
+ 68,000	+4,000	+ 624,000	– 6,000
+ 499,200		– 68,000	
– 40,000			
– 297,000		– 499,200	
– 30,800		+ 124,800	
– 8,000			
– 88,000			
– 5,000			
– 40,000			
+ 40,000			
– 3,200			
– 3,640	**Inventory finished goods**		
– 2,400	**+ 18,000**		
– 13,000	+ 320,000		
– 6,000	– 312,000		
– 4,000	+ 22,000		
– 12,000	– 4,000		
– 3,120			
+ 53,640	**Depreciation**		
	– 4,800		
Inventory raw materials	– 2,400		
	– 520		
+ 16,000	– 4,800	**Prepaid expenses**	
+ 330,000	**– 12,520**	**+ 1,000**	
– 320,000		– 1,000	
– 800		0	
+ 25,200			

Assets

Fixed assets

+ 48,000	**Intangible assets**
+ 40,000	—
+ 3,640	+ 6,000
+ 80,000	
+171,640	

TOTAL ASSETS

388,760

Liabilities

Accounts Payable	**Accruals**	**Long-Term Debt**
+ 40,000	+ 11,120	—
− 40,000	+ 2,800	
+ 330,000	− 8,000	
− 297,000	+ 8,000	+ 80,000
+ 33,000	− 3,120	
	+ 47,355	
	+ 58,155	

TOTAL LIABILITIES

$171,155

Capital

Common Stock	Retained Earnings
+ 80,000	+ 17,680
+ 40,000	+ 624,000
+ 120,000	– 312,000
	– 30,800
	– 2,800
	– 88,000
	– 8,000
	– 1,000
	– 5,000
	– 3,200
	– 2,400
	– 520
	– 4,800
	– 6,000
	– 800
	– 4,000
	– 2,400
	– 13,000
	– 12,000
	– 47,355
	+ 97,605

TOTAL CAPITAL

$217,605

TOTAL LIABILITIES AND CAPITAL

$388,760

Acme Widget Company Balance Sheet End of Second Year of Operations

ASSETS			LIABILITIES AND CAPITAL		
CURRENT ASSETS	**Year Two**	**Year One**	**CURRENT LIABILITIES**	**Year Two**	**Year One**
Cash	$53,640	$2,600	Accounts payable	$33,000	$40,000
Marketable securities	4,000	—	Accruals	58,155	11,120
Accounts receivable	124,800	68,000	**Total current liabilities**	91,155	51,120
Less reserve for doubtful accounts	– 6,000	—			
Net accounts receivable	118,800	68,000	LONG-TERM LIABILITIES		
Inventory			Long-term debt	80,000	—
Raw materials	25,200	16,000	Total long-term liabilities	80,000	—
Finished goods	22,000	18,000	TOTAL LIABILITIES	$171,155	$51,120
Total inventory	47,200	34,000			
Prepaid expenses	0	1,000	CAPITAL		
Total current assets	223,640	105,600	Common stock	120,000	80,000
NONCURRENT ASSETS			Retained earnings	97,605	17,680
Fixed assets	171,640	48,000	TOTAL CAPITAL	$217,605	$97,680
Less depreciation	12,520	4,800			
Net fixed assets	159,120	43,200	TOTAL LIABILITIES AND CAPITAL	$388,760	$148,800
Intangible assets	6,000	—			
Total noncurrent assets	165,120	43,200			
TOTAL ASSETS	$388,760	$148,800			

Acme Widget Company Comparative Income Statement for Year Two

Item	Year Two	Percentage of Sales	Year One	Percentage of Sales
Sales	$624,000	100.0%	$292,000	100.0%
Cost of sales	316,800	50.8	146,000	50.0
Gross profit	307,200	49.2	146,000	50.0
Salaries	129,600	20.8	96,000	32.9
Advertising	13,000	2.1	10,000	3.4
Machinery depreciation	4,800	0.8	4,800	1.6
Furniture and fixture depreciation	520	0.0	—	—
Building occupancy costs	8,400	1.3	12,000	4.1
Office expenses	2,400	0.4	2,400	0.8
Reserve	6,000	1.0	—	—
Total operating expenses	164,720	26.4	125,200	42.9
Operating profit	142,480	22.8	20,800	7.1
Nonoperating income and expenses	(3,200)	0.1	—	—
Net profit before taxes	139,280	22.3	20,800	7.1
Income taxes	47,355	7.6	3,120	1.1
Net profit after taxes	$91,925	14.7%	$17,680	6.1%

Acme Fluted Widget Machine Purchase Decision

Assumptions:

- *Profit*

Year	Units Sold	× Price Per Unit	= Sales	– Expenses)	= Profit
1	14,000	$9.50	$133,000	$128,400	$4,600
2	18,000	9.60	172,800	154,800	18,000
3	20,000	9.70	194,000	168,000	26,000
4	20,000	9.70	194,000	168,000	26,000
Total	72,000		$693,800	$619,200	$74,600

Note: Expenses = $4.40 raw materials + $2.20 in variable operating expenses for each unit, plus $36,000 operator's salary. (All these costs might need to be adjusted for likely inflation, as could the selling price. And taxes are ignored.)

- *Time.* Four years (could be more or less).
- *Interest rate.* 6% (could be the 4% rate or a much higher rate; I arbitrarily chose 6%).

Discounted Cash Flow

Cash Paid Out				Cash Received		
Year	Amount ×	Present Value Factor =	Present Value	Amount ×	Present Value Factor =	Present Value
0	$72,000	1.000	$72,000	$—	—	—
1	—	—	—	4,600	.9434	$4,340
2	—	—	—	18,000	.8900	16,020
3	—	—	—	26,000	.8396	21,830
4	—	—	—	26,000	.7921	20,595
Total	$72,000		$72,000	$74,600		$62,785

Acme Widget Year Two Statement of Changes In Financial Position

Sources of working capital

Net profit after taxes	$91,925
Depreciation	7,720
Total from operations	99,645
Stock issued	40,000
Long-term borrowing	80,000
Total sources of working capital	219,645

Uses of working capital	
Purchase of fixed assets	123,640
Purchase of intangible assets	6,000
Dividends paid	12,000
Reduction in long-term debt	0
Stock purchased	0
Total uses of working capital	141,640

Increase in working capital	78,005
Changes in working capital	
Cash and marketable securities	55,040
Accounts receivable, net after reserve	50,800
Inventory, net after write-down	13,200
Prepaid expenses	(1,000)
Accounts payable	7,000
Accruals	(47,035)
	78,005
Working capital at beginning of year	54,480
Working capital at end of year	132,485

Acme Widget Year Three

Acme Widget Company Cash Flow Budget for Year Three

	Jan.	Feb.	Mar.	Apr.	May
Sales of Regular Widgets	$55,000	55,000	55,000	55,000	55,000
Sales of Fluted Widgets	—	—	—	—	9,500
Total Sales	55,000	55,000	55,000	55,000	64,500
Collections—Previous Year	47,520	47,520	23,760	—	—
Collections—Current Year	—	—	55,000	55,000	55,000
Total Collections	47,520	47,520	78,760	55,000	55,000
Inventory Payments— Previous Year	33,000	—	—	—	—
Inventory Payments— Current Year Regular	—	27,500	27,500	27,500	27,500
Inventory Payments— Current Year Fluted	—	—	—	—	—
Total Inventory Payments	33,000	27,500	27,500	27,500	27,500
Office Expenses and Interest	733	733	733	733	733
Advertising	—	3,000	—	4,000	3,000
Salaries and Bonus	10,800	10,800	10,800	13,800	13,800
Tax Payment	—	—	47,355	—	—
Fluted Widget Machine Payment	—	—	72,000	—	—
Dividend Payment	—	—	—	—	—
TOTAL CASH PAID OUT	44,533	42,033	158,388	93,388	46,033
TOTAL CASH IN	47,520	47,520	78,760	55,000	55,000
NET CASH FLOW	2,987	5,487	(79,628)	8,967	9,967
Cash on Hand—Beginning	57,640	60,627	66,114	(13,514)	(4,547)
Cash on Hand—Ending	60,627	66,114	(13,514)	(4,547)	5,420
Additional Cash Needed			13,514		

Jun.	Jul.	Aug.	Sep.	Oct.	Nov.	Dec.	Total
55,000	$44,000	44,000	66,000	66,000	55,000	55,000	$660,000
11,400	15,200	14,250	19,000	19,950	19,950	23,750	133,000
66,400	59,200	58,250	85,000	85,950	74,950	78,750	793,000
—	—	—	—	—	—	—	118,800
55,000	64,500	66,400	59,200	58,250	85,000	85,950	639,300
55,000	64,500	66,400	59,200	58,250	85,000	85,950	758,100
—	—	—	—	—	—	—	33,000
27,500	27,500	22,000	22,000	33,000	33,000	27,500	302,500
4,400	5,280	7,040	6,600	8,800	9,240	9,240	50,600
31,900	32,780	29,040	28,600	41,800	42,240	36,740	386,100
733	733	733	733	733	733	733	8,796
—	—	—	—	—	3,000	—	13,000
13,800	13,800	13,800	13,800	13,800	13,800	23,800	166,600
—	—	—	—	—	—	—	47,355
—	—	—	—	—	—	—	72,000
—	—	—	—	—	—	12,000	12,000
46,433	47,313	43,573	43,133	56,333	59,773	73,273	705,851
55,000	64,500	66,400	59,200	58,250	85,000	85,950	758,100
8,567	17,187	22,827	16,067	1,917	25,227	12,677	52,249
5,420	13,987	31,174	54,001	70,068	71,985	97,212	57,640
13,987	31,174	54,001	70,068	71,985	97,212	109,889	109,889

B

Present Value Tables

The formula for present value is

$$P = \frac{1}{(1 + i)^n}$$

where P = present value, i = interest rate, and n = number of years.

The Present Value of $1.00

	Interest Rate							
Number of Years	**5%**	**6%**	**7%**	**8%**	**9%**	**10%**	**11%**	**12%**
1	.9524	.9434	.9346	.9259	.9174	.9091	.9009	.8929
2	.9070	.8900	.8734	.8573	.8417	.8264	.8116	.7972
3	.8638	.8396	.8163	.7938	.7722	.7513	.7312	.7118
4	.8227	.7921	.7629	.7350	.7084	.6830	.6587	.6355
5	.7835	.7473	.7130	.6806	.6499	.6209	.5935	.5674
6	.7462	.7050	.6663	.6302	.5963	.5645	.5346	.5066
7	.7107	.6651	.6227	.5835	.5470	.5132	.4817	.4523
8	.6768	.6274	.5820	.5403	.5019	.4665	.4339	.4039
9	.6446	.5919	.5439	.5002	.4604	.4241	.3909	.3606
10	.6139	.5584	.5083	.4632	.4224	.3855	.3522	.3220
11	.5847	.5268	.4751	.4289	.3875	.3505	.3173	.2875
12	.5568	.4970	.4440	.3971	.3555	.3186	.2858	.2567
13	.5303	.4688	.4150	.3677	.3262	.2897	.2575	.2292
14	.5051	.4423	.3878	.3405	.2992	.2633	.2320	.2046
15	.4810	.4173	.3624	.3152	.2745	.2394	.2090	.1827
16	.4581	.3936	.3387	.2919	.2519	.2176	.1883	.1631
17	.4363	.3714	.3166	.2703	.2311	.1978	.1696	.1456
18	.4155	.3503	.2959	.2502	.2120	.1799	.1528	.1300
19	.3957	.3305	.2765	.2317	.1945	.1635	.1377	.1161
20	.3769	.3118	.2584	.2145	.1784	.1486	.1241	.1037

The Present Value of $1.00, Continued

Interest Rate

Number of Years	13%	14%	15%	16%	17%	18%	19%	20%
1	.8850	.8772	.8696	.8621	.8547	.8475	.8403	.8333
2	.7831	.7695	.7561	.7432	.7305	.7182	.7062	.6944
3	.6931	.6750	.6575	.6407	.6244	.6086	.5934	.5787
4	.6133	.5921	.5718	.5523	.5336	.5158	.4987	.4823
5	.5428	.5194	.4972	.4761	.4561	.4371	.4190	.4019
6	.4803	.4556	.4323	.4104	.3898	.3704	.3521	.3349
7	.4251	.3996	.3759	.3538	.3332	.3139	.2959	.2791
8	.3762	.3506	.3269	.3050	.2848	.2660	.2487	.2326
9	.3329	.3075	.2843	.2630	.2434	.2255	.2090	.1938
10	.2946	.2697	.2472	.2267	.2080	.1911	.1756	.1615
11	.2607	.2366	.2149	.1954	.1778	.1619	.1476	.1346
12	.2307	.2076	.1869	.1685	.1520	.1372	.1240	.1122
13	.2042	.1821	.1625	.1452	.1299	.1163	.1042	.0935
14	.1807	.1597	.1413	.1252	.1110	.0985	.0876	.0779
15	.1599	.1401	.1229	.1079	.0949	.0835	.0736	.0649
16	.1415	.1229	.1069	.0930	.0811	.0708	.0618	.0541
17	.1252	.1078	.0929	.0802	.0693	.0600	.0520	.0451
18	.1108	.0946	.0808	.0691	.0592	.0508	.0437	.0376
19	.0981	.0829	.0703	.0596	.0506	.0431	.0367	.0313
20	.0868	.0728	.0611	.0514	.0433	.0365	.0308	.0261

Index

FT Press

FINANCIAL TIMES

In an increasingly competitive world, it is quality
of thinking that gives an edge—an idea that opens new
doors, a technique that solves a problem, or an insight
that simply helps make sense of it all.

We work with leading authors in the various arenas
of business and finance to bring cutting-edge thinking
and best-learning practices to a global market.

It is our goal to create world-class print publications
and electronic products that give readers
knowledge and understanding that can then be
applied, whether studying or at work.

To find out more about our business
products, you can visit us at www.ftpress.com.